Offending girls

Studies in Society

Titles include:

Offending girls

sex, youth and justice

Kerry Carrington

Allen & Unwin

First published in 1993 by
Allen & Unwin Pty Ltd
9 Atchison Street, St Leonards, NSW 2065 Australia

National Library of Australia
Cataloguing-in-Publication entry:

Carrington, Kerry.
 Offending girls: sex, youth and justice.

 Bibliography.
 Includes index.
 ISBN 1 86373 523 2.

 1. Delinquent girls–Australia. 2. Juvenile justice,
 Administration of–Australia. I. Title.
 (Series: Studies in society (Sydney, NSW)).

364.36

Set in 10/11 Times Roman by DOCUPRO, Sydney
Printed by SRM Production Services Sdn Bhd, Malaysia

10 9 8 7 6 5 4 3 2 1

*This book is dedicated to the memory of
the late Julienne Vennard*

Contents

Figures and Tables

Figures

Tables

Abbreviations

ABS	Australian Bureau of Statistics
AGPS	Australian Government Printing Service
B file	A ward file
CAP	Community Aid Panel
DO	District Officer
IB file	Criminal dossier
JCI	Juvenile Criminal Index
LGA	Local Government Area
NSW	New South Wales
Qld	Queensland
SA	South Australia
Vic	Victoria
WA	Western Australia
YACS	The Department of Youth and Community Services NSW (also referred to as the department)
YOST	Young offender support team

Acknowledgments

I am immensely grateful to what in 1986 was called the Department of Youth and Community Services and its Minister Frank Walker, for granting special permission to access their confidential archives and to Special Magistrate Rod Blackmore for allowing the observations of Children's Courts' proceedings. Not many government agencies have the courage to allow an independent researcher access to confidential files and proceedings which go to the heart of their organisation and the way they manage their clients. In particular I wish to thank Laurie Young, Liz Moore and Garth Luke from the department for their support of this project at the time. Thankyou also to all those people from the department who assisted in the initial stages of this research, particularly Kerry and David from Adoptions, Andy the caretaker at Kambala and Johno from Records. Variations of some of the material and arguments in the book have been previously published in several journals in editions now out of print and I would like to acknowledge the support of the editors of *Law in Context, The Australian and New Zealand Journal of Criminology* and *The Journal of Social Justice Studies* in publishing those earlier papers.

I am especially grateful to my PhD supervisors, Professors Bob Connell and Rachel Sharp, who patiently guided me throughout the research process to its fruition. I would also like to thank David Brown from the University of NSW Law School for his helpful advice and comments on drafts of the manuscript. I am indeed indebted to The Australian Sociological Association for presenting me with the Jean Martin Award and to Allen & Unwin for publishing this book as the winner of that award. It certainly would not have had an Australian-based publisher otherwise. I have a long list of other friends and family members to thank for their continuing support over the many years—including five siblings and two sets of parents. My mother, Jess, however deserves a special mention for her embarrassingly loyal support throughout my tertiary education. I also owe a special debt to Paul McCarthy from Griffith University for his encouragement of a 'wild surfie girl' in her first year of university. Thanks to Paul, I swapped the wild surf for a universe of wild ideas.

In vital respects I feel that this book, although supposedly sole-authored, has many authors. While I accept full responsibility for its shortcomings, many of the innovative ideas which appear in the text are the product of intellectual exchanges with Russell Hogg, my husband, friend and continuing source of intellectual inspiration, and with some of my colleagues especially Barry Morris, Gill Cowlishaw, Gay Hawkins, Debbie Tyler, Gary Wickham and Pieter Degeling. I am also grateful to Ellen Jordan for assistance with the research for Chapter 3. To my adorable children, Amie and Rosa I am especially thankful for their forbearance and understanding during the process of writing this manuscript.

Glossary

Essentialism

Essentialism is a form of analysis in which social phenomena are understood not in terms of the specific conditions of their existence, but in terms of some presumed essence or interest (Hindess, 1977, p. 95). Thus membership of a social category (i.e. women, working class) is understood to produce certain shared interests even if these are not recognised by the members themselves. These shared interests are said to be the necessary objective effects of a pre-given social structure or essence. This is then said to provide a more real and fundamental framework of analysis than members own attitudes and conceptions of their own interests. Essentialism therefore imposes a unity upon its object of inquiry by assuming that members of a social group have similar interests (i.e. women, blacks, workers).

Gender essentialism

Gender essentialism is defined as:

> . . . the notion that a unitary, 'essential' women's experience can be
> isolated and described independently of race, class, sexual
> orientation, and other realities of experience. (Harris, 1990, p. 585)

The shared experiences of sex subordination are said to make it meaningful to adopt essentialist positions and to speak with authority about 'women as a group'. Gender essentialism can be detected in accounts of universal female oppression, as well as in appeals to a female essence, because both impose a unity upon its object of inquiry, women (Fuss, 1989, p. 2). The flip side of this is the attribution of a shared masculinist interest to all men, or to certain institutions such as the state or the law which are regarded as patriarchal in essence or nature.

Discourse
Discourses are the frameworks of knowledge and power which delineate the conditions of the possibility of speaking and writing. Discourse is not just how we speak to one another, although it can be, it is more a question of what is sayable and what gets counted as truth. One of the major aims of discourse analysis is to examine how the social body is governed through the production of 'truth'. It analyses the shifts and disruptions in the order of discourse (what gets counted as knowledge) that circulate in internal regimes of power in specific sites and their knowledge effects (Foucault, 1981). Discourse analysis stresses the discontinuity of discourses, their disruptive and productive effects, their plurality and their dispersion throughout the social body and across the social spectrum.

Governmentality
Governmentality is the art of government which can be described simply as 'the conduct of conduct' (Gordon, 1991, p. 2). Government necessarily involves the calculation of problems (particularly of problem populations) which may arise and how they can be managed (Wickham, 1992). Governmentality is not just an activity of the state and its agencies, although it certainly can be. While the state is one of the instruments of government, governmentality operates in a variety of limited domains, among which the family, the school and the workplace are important.

Power
Power is conceived not as an object which some have and some do not have, but as an effect which is exercised primarily through technical rather than coercive means and particularly through the control of knowledge. While its exercise can be repressive it can also be positive. Power is largely an impersonal matter which does not depend on the occurrence of personal interaction between two or more parties. It might be useful to consider how architectural arrangements, for example, govern the possibilities of existence and thus create power effects without personal interaction. A well-known example of this is the architectural device known as the panopticon which is used widely in the management of populations in schools, hospitals, factories and prisons. The panopticon, by creating the illusion of constant surveillance, generates the power effect of being watched. Power while omnipresent, is never fixed or totalising (Foucault, 1981)

Policing
The term policing is not used in this text in a totalising reductivist
way to mean social control. Nor is it meant to be interpreted in a
simple negative sense, as the policing of person, family and popu-
lace in ways commensurate with the practice of government,
although it can be. It is rather more complex. Policing is one of the
arts of governmentality—the institution and dispersion of norms of
conduct and their social administration concerned with the formation
of the 'good order of a population' (Pasquino, 1991, p. 111).

1   Introduction

State wards comprise about one fifth of all girls processed by the Children's Courts. Most of the girls recruited into the official delinquent population come from large, materially impoverished families living in either housing commission estates or Aboriginal communities. Many of thse girls are before the courts for non-criminal behaviour for which adults cannot be punished, for example running away from home or being abused by their guardians. Almost half of their siblings have also been processed by the courts as delinquent youth. Those who are most severely punished by the courts are not girls apprehended for criminal offences, but rather those considered 'predelinquent' and 'in need of care'. There is a steady flow of young bodies between the state institutions set up to care for the abused child and the juvenile detention centres set up to correct the abusive child. What I am describing here is a highly selective delinquency manufacturing process that is the product of a complex web of modern governmental technologies primarily designed to save children from 'bad' families. This book is a study of these particular governmental technologies. Its central objective is to explore how female delinquency is manufactured by the juvenile justice system itself.

While this text is a criminological study of sorts it neither seeks to answer aetiological questions or offer any correctional 'solutions' for 'offending girls', nor does it aim to represent the views of such girls, important though these might be. Rather it is a study of the administration of juvenile justice, its nexus with the provision of child welfare, the forms of knowledge and power that produce this delinquency manufacturing process and its highly selective penetration into the social body which make girls from Aboriginal communities and housing commission estates the most likely candidates for entry into the official delinquent population.

Youth is a passage through which all adults in the social body must invariably pass and the government of youth through this passage is absolutely crucial to the kind of citizenry comprising that social body. This is one reason why adolescence is such an intense period of regulation, experienced by those subject to such regulation as being double-edged. While intense scrutiny may be repressive for young people, their government through school and family is probably what insulates most of them from the carceral reaches of juvenile justice. Youth is also a metaphor for trouble and a time for the frivolous pursuit of sex, lust and pleasure. Understandably very few pass through it without having technically committed acts of delinquency, such as under-age drinking, smoking dope, illicit sex, shop-lifting, truanting and so on. Of course there are significant gender differences in the profile of adolescent offending. Nevertheless relatively few young people (although four times as many boys as girls) are actually channelled into the hands of the justice authorities from this large cohort of potential recruits to the State's official delinquent population. What is interesting is that the few who do end up in the juvenile justice system are highly concentrated in identifiable sections of the social body demarcated from the general population by their poverty and welfare dependence.

For those unfamiliar with the juvenile justice systems in countries like Australia, Britain and the United States, it is important to understand that there are two major avenues through which children and young people may be brought before a Children's Court. On the one hand, children who have reached the age of criminal responsibility (usually 10 years) may be charged with a criminal offence in much the same way as an adult. On the other hand, children of any age (usually up to 18 years) may be brought before the court on what are commonly referred to as care matters, but which are also known as welfare matters or status offences (such as neglect, abuse, destitution, uncontrollability, truancy). Despite the distinction between criminal grounds and ostensibly protective grounds for coercive intervention in the lives of children, the manner in which they have been processed through the Children's Courts and managed in institutional forms of care and control have not been clearly differentiated. In many cases, children before the courts for their own protection are detained in the same institutions as juvenile offenders. In any case, the use of separate institutions for children in need of protection (i.e. state ward establishments) does not mean that these institutions differ significantly from juvenile prisons in their level of internal security and organisation of their internal daily regime. It is in this context that committal to state care has a life long association with punishment for some of those who have passed through it. This is why some girls identify 'the welfare' as 'the enemy' and prefer a committal to a juvenile prison to a committal to a state ward establishment.

Child welfare and juvenile justice have never constituted wholly separate domains in the formal legal sense, let alone in their day-to-day administration. While recent reforms have attempted to separate welfare cases from criminal cases the nexus between the two still exists because the mundane daily management of the abused child and the abusive child relies on similar forms of knowledge and power. This is the main argument developed in this book.

The basis of the argument is divided into six discrete chapters, each concerned with specific issues but connected by an overall argument about forms of knowledge and power that regulate young people. The book's central concern concentrates on the forms of government, knowledge and power that operate over girls (and their families) who are channelled into the reaches of the child welfare and juvenile justice authorities. The first two chapters clear the ground for the development of such an argument by deconstructing two different but popular structuralist readings of juvenile justice. Chapter 2 takes issue with an argument widely accepted in the international feminist literature, and often referred to as the sexualisation thesis, that girls who appear before the Children's Courts do so predominantly because of their sexual conduct. Sexual conduct is indeed an important factor in the manufacture of female delinquency, but not necessarily in the way that is implied by the sexualisation thesis. Chapter 3 addresses specific aspects of the relationship between Aboriginal girls and the justice authorities. It attempts to provide an explanation for their massive rates of criminalisation compared with non-Aboriginal girls. However, I have resisted the temptation to replace a structuralist reading of gender and justice with one of race and justice. Rather I have tried to analyse how deviation from the cultural specificity of social norms is translated into a logic of government which produces delinquency in the image of otherness, in this case Aboriginality.

The remaining four chapters then set out to offer a reading (in some cases a number of readings) of the way in which female delinquency is manufactured by the juvenile justice authorities. Chapters 4, 5 and 6 examine the principal sites through which the girls in my study were channelled into the hands of the justice agencies. The reason for organising the book in this way was to escape the legal common sense view that the Children's Court is the focal point of the justice system around which all other decision-making processes revolve. Chapter 4 focuses on the school as one of these important sites. It analyses the overlap between judicial and educational forms of power and asks why schools do not do more to insulate truants from the often futile and repressive interventions of juvenile justice. Chapter 5 looks at the family as another principal site from which children and young people are channelled into the juvenile justice system. It describes and analyses what happens to families who fail to govern their children in ways desired by the welfare agencies and justice authorities. It also documents what happens to girls who, through no fault of their own, pass into the hands of these agencies either because of inadequate family support or because of abuse. Chapter 6 examines the policing of youth culture as another site from which girls (but many more boys) are channelled into the juvenile justice system. It offers several different readings of this delinquency manufacturing process, using the theoretical frameworks of cultural studies, feminism and post-structuralism.

It has been commonplace to conceive the administration of juvenile justice in terms of a series of tensions between welfare and justice. The final chapter takes issue with the terms of this wearisome debate. It provides an account of the mechanics of the criminalisation process through which the girls in my study and their families were processed and seeks to provide an answer, however partial, to the vulnerability of some girls to the gaze of the justice authorities, and the immunity of others. This leads me to one last point by way of a general introduction to the text.

One of the major themes developed in the book is that girls are not a homogeneous lot subject to a seamless web of male oppression. They are noticeably differentiated in their vulnerability to the repressive forms of regulation that operate through juvenile justice. Any unity imposed upon 'girls as a group' and their treatment by the justice authorities is a fictive one.

Methodology

The research for this book is based on a doctorate I completed in the Department of Sociology at Macquarie University in 1989. The research design incorporated three empirical data collecting techniques undertaken in the following order: a random sample of 1046 records of girls born between the years 1960 to 1964 taken from the NSW Juvenile Criminal Index (JCI); a study of the criminal dossiers, ward files and case notes of fifty-nine girls from that sample, most of whom were considered by the authorities as chronic 're-offenders'; an observational study of several Children's Courts in metropolitan Sydney (for detail see Carrington, 1989, pp. 64–87). The method of each of these is outlined briefly below.

The random sample from the JCI of 1046 girls born in the years 1960 through 1964 constitutes 10 per cent of all such records (Fig. 1.1). In principle, the index holds one card for every male and female juvenile who has ever appeared in any New South Wales Children's Court jurisdiction. The records remain active until the person attains the age of eighteen years and additions are entered for consecutive court appearances. When the records become inactive they are filed alphabetically into boxes, indexed according to the year of birth and then (in theory) sent to State Archives. It

Figure 1.1 Sampling methodology

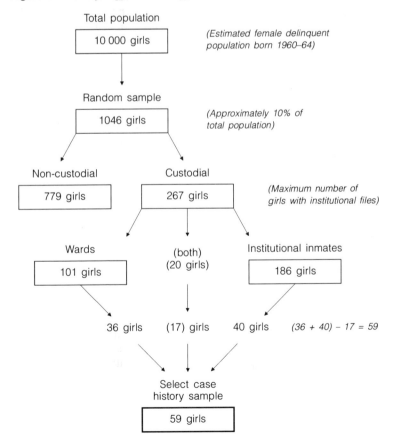

was the most recently inactive JCI records at the time of the data collection which formed the total population of the random sample. A total of sixty variables was coded for each JCI record, including such information as year of birth, place of residence, history of offences and court outcomes for each of the 1046 girls. A great deal of empirical data produced by this method has not been included in the book, simply because it duplicates the picture of female court appearances produced by official statistics. This material is in the thesis for those who are particularly interested. The most important data generated by the statistical procedure was information about place of residence which made it possible to calculate a female delinquency detection rate for each local government area (LGA) within the State of NSW and to then correlate this rate with Australian Bureau of Statistics (ABS) social indices.

I then read the criminal dossiers of fifty-nine of the 1046 girls from the larger sample who, on average had appeared before the Children's Court five times each during their youth. The selection

Figure 1.2   Selection of case studies

	Institutional inmates	wards	(both)		girls
A	186	101	(20)	=	267

Name sought from B card index

	Institutional inmates	wards	(both)		girls
B	186	60	(20)	=	226

B Number located from B card index

	Institutional inmates	wards	(both)		girls
C	108	45	(17)	=	136

Located retrieval number from IB or B File indexes

	Institutional inmates	wards	(both)		girls
D	53	40	(17)	=	76

Dossiers retrieved from State archives

	Institutional inmates	wards	(both)		girls
E	40	36	(17)	=	59

of the cases was largely a practical matter, but in principal I tried to locate the files of girls with long criminal histories. Initially I had asked for most of the files of the girls from the larger sample who had been taken into State custody either as wards or institutional inmates (Fig. 1.2). Through a process of attrition I ended up with only fifty-nine from a possible 267 of such cases out of the 1046. The files assemble in chronological order a collection of documents produced about each girl and her family by the juvenile justice and child welfare agencies. In departmental terminology the documents are called B files for State wards and IB files for institutional inmates. As it turned out there was considerable overlap between the two as thirty-six of the fifty-nine girls had both kinds of files, and many of the institutional inmates had been placed in ward establishments and vice versa. It was then that I decided to dispense with departmental terminology preferring to call the files case notes, or dossiers as they are in this book. There was an average of 150 documents in each dossier, although the largest dossier contained in excess of 800 documents and the smallest fifteen. In total I read more than 8000 documents transcribing at least 80 per cent of their contents to avoid the trap of selective note-taking. This took the better part of a year.

The dossiers include court reports, psychological and medical assessments, conference reports, home reports, ward reports, sworn statements, official documents of the Children's Court, police facts sheets and so on. This book quotes heavily from such sources, most of them in full. It is important to note that documents of this sort do not necessarily record what actually happened. Rather, as Cicourel suggests, the routine organisational processes that produce them make the dossiers intensely political sources of information (Cicourel, 1968, p. xiii). Official documents of the sort I read therefore tend to normalise actions taken by the authorities in specific instances as the legitimate treatment of a case, regardless of what actually happened (Garfinkel, 1967, pp. 202–3). They often justify what should happen (i.e. court reports) or what should have happened (probation reports) or what was said (i.e. records of interview). The records of interviews were notorious in this respect as many were written after the event. Only the most crude positivist would attempt a literal reading of these texts. This is why I do not privilege such documents as being the impartial bearers of truth but rather see them as the products of a specific governmental process. I have attempted to read them in a number of possible ways: I do not claim that these readings are exhaustive, impartial or error-free, but they are the best possible at present that I could do.

The research process was greatly affected by ethical considerations and my access to both the Juvenile Criminal Index and the dossiers was carried out under strict departmental supervision. Ironically, the office allotted to my use was formerly a cell of Parramatta Girls' Industrial School, more recently known as Kambala, an institution for delinquent girls located alongside the Parramatta women's jail.

Since these documents carry a one hundred year embargo approval to research and publish the results of my findings was sought and granted by the Department of Youth and Community Services (YACS). Since that time the department has undergone a number of name changes variously referred to in the text. For the sake of ease I simply refer to it as the department. Approval for access was granted under the condition that no individual girl, family or employee could be identified through the publication of my research. I have undertaken considerable efforts to guarantee anonymity by using pseudonyms, by systematically altering dates and places and by omitting individually identifying information where necessary.

The final research procedure involved a series of observations of a number of Sydney metropolitan Children's Courts, which ostensibly did not amount to the collection of much empirical data. Since Children's Courts are closed courts, permission to conduct this research was sought from and granted by the Senior Special Magistrate of Metropolitan Children's Courts, Mr Rod Blackmore. I undertook a stratified sample of observations over a five week period, Monday the first week, Tuesday the second and so on until I had completed one week of observations in each court. While the fruits of this method are not readily apparent in the text, upon reflection the observations were essential to arriving at the understanding that the Children's Court is not necessarily the centre of the justice process, and may only be peripheral to it. In other words, the Children's Court does *not* necessarily exercise sovereignty over the justice system. The significance of this formulation has been crucial to the argument developed in this book to account for the manufacture of female delinquency by the justice system itself.

2   Feminist readings of female delinquency

The defence of or challenge to gender essentialism has become a major focus of contention in feminist criminology as it has in feminist theory more generally.[1] This chapter challenges the veracity of essentialist feminist readings of female delinquency which have emerged during the last two decades to explain sex differences in juvenile court statistics. I suggest an alternative feminist reading which does not reduce the processing of girls in the justice system to the effect of one underlying unitary discourse (i.e. patriarchy). As a way of developing the argument I take up the case of a sexually active girl whose conduct became the subject of considerable court action. I will call her Judy although this is not her real name.

Judy's case notes

Between the ages of fifteen and seventeen years, Judy appeared before the Children's Court on six separate occasions for matters involving welfare complaints. These are matters which relate to non-criminal conduct. She appeared twice for being uncontrollable, once for being destitute, once for breaching probation, once for absconding from a ward establishment and once for being exposed to moral danger. On three occasions she was committed to an institution and on another occasion she was made a ward of the State.[2]

At the time of first recorded contact with the juvenile justice authorities, Judy lived in a complicated extended family arrangement. As a baby, her mother died, leaving her in the care of distant relatives. Judy then spent the remainder of her childhood living between the homes of two related foster families. She first appeared before the Children's Court charged with being exposed to moral danger after running away from one of these homes. Judy apparently told the district officer that she was caught smoking at school and feared being beaten with a stockwhip if she returned home (Court Report, 17 July 1979). On this occasion the court released her on a period of probation for twelve months. A couple of weeks later Judy again ran away from home, but was apprehended by the school counsellor who immediately escorted her to the district office where she was later interviewed. The information that emerged during the interview, quoted below, formed the basis of the complaint that Judy had breached her terms of probation.

> On Thursday, Judy ran away from school and was missing over night until located by Mrs Y (the school counsellor) on the 4th August 79.
> A lengthy interview was held with the girl at this office on the 4th August but she continually refused to return home and boasted quite freely of her activities with members of the opposite sex. The alternatives were carefully pointed out to Judy but she maintained her attitude and refused to return home. She stated that she felt her sister was favoured more than she was. She stated that there had been more advances from John (her step-brother) and that this was not her problem at home. She stated that she felt she was not allowed enough freedom at home and also that she was harassed on the school bus. She stated that on Wednesday this week some boys had taken her comb and refused to return it until she undid her blouse revealing her breasts to them. She said that she had complied with this but agreed that she had not had to do this and that she had been a party to misconduct on the school bus. She further agreed that her foster mother had been advised of this behaviour and knew what had been transpiring by Wednesday evening and this had not made Judy popular at home. Judy further agreed that her reputation for engaging in sexual activities was becoming well known in the area and that she had, herself, encouraged this (to) a very large extent.
> The girl was brought from a remand shelter on 9th August 1979 to appear before a Special Court for Remand purposes and she again refused to return home. Mrs X (foster mother) stated that she felt the girl did not want to be restricted in her activities at all but wished to be allowed to do as she chose, and that this had been the case when she lived at (another foster home) when she was allowed more freedom.
> Mr and Mrs X state that they can no longer control the girl and fear for the consequences of her continuing to behave in the manner she had demonstrated over the past few months. The girl refuses to

return home and there are no other relatives willing to accept her care. It is also of further interest that the girls were not aware of their true status (as foster children) until recent times and this has no doubt contributed to Judy's unsettled behaviour. Judy has had an unfortunate upbringing in that she has been subject to molestation by people whom she should have been able to trust but in spite of intensive efforts to assist the girl since her last appearance at Court she refuses to behave in an acceptable manner and has indicated that she wishes to be allowed her freedom and not be restricted.

In all the circumstances, particularly in view of her attitude, I feel that Judy should be committed in general terms where efforts can be made in a controlled situation to rectify some of the damage that has already been done. *Recommendation*: Committal to an Institution. (Court Report, 10 August 1979)

On the day that Judy was to appear in court, a family who had previously cared for her agreed to do so again. In view of this she was given a suspended committal for a period of eighteen months. Upon her release, Judy was closely supervised by the district officer who instigated a series of regular (and often unannounced) visits to her home and school.[3] Two months into her suspended committal Judy appeared before the Children's Court charged with being uncontrollable after failing to return home one night. Before setting out the reasons for taking court action, the Court Report prepared by the supervising district officer provided a summary of Judy's family background, a description of the family home, financial situation and details of Judy's two previous court appearances. The Court Report then rationalised Judy's committal to an institution in the following terms:

[Judy] settled well initially. After the honeymoon period, however, the pressures started to build for Judy. There was confusion . . . there was loneliness . . . there were difficulties settling into a new school and area where unfortunately her previous reputation became known; and probably most of all the attempts in mid-adolescence to sort out all the emotional bondings in her life. Judy began to rebel against school although truancy was not a feature and it was decided that if she could find a job she could be exempted. She was unsuccessful in these efforts and there suddenly commenced an acceleration of local gossip about Judy and her activities and proclivities which most likely was a fair mixture of fact and fiction. No real misbehaviour became apparent until 27/9/79 when she stayed out until 2 a.m. after a bashing from a local girl. After that were a couple of incidents of late arrival home which were not reported to me, and then on 8/10/79 she left home in the afternoon and did not return. She contacted X (her foster brother) the following morning however, was very distressed and asked him to bring her home. She claimed to have just walked around most of the night just thinking. On this occasion she was reminded of the conditions of the Court Order during the course of another counselling interview, and she was therefore given one more chance. The School Counsellor also had a long interview with Judy in the following week and thought that progress was being made by Judy in her attitudes and self-evaluation.

However, the following Saturday Judy failed to arrive home after a day spent with her natural father and was finally found by police when she was walking along the road on Monday morning. I have not had an opportunity to talk to Judy since then but I am in no doubt that the lass is in desperate need of some time to break her present cycle of behaviour and also to reinforce that Orders of the Court are not to be treated lightly. I think that essentially she is a kind girl who is desperate for acceptance but is seeking this acceptance in ways that will damage her irreparably. I would imagine that at the moment her self-esteem is about as low as it will ever get.

There are no other relatives in a position to take Judy but in any case one could not see such a solution being helpful as it would only add to her confusion. A voluntary placement is not possible because of her age and lack of job skills. She has no real ambition but is gifted in Art and Craft work. It is felt that committal to a training school would serve Judy's best interests at this stage as the controlled environment would curb her impulsive behaviour and afford protection whilst she gains some extra maturity.
Recommendation: Committal to an Institution. (Court Report, 20 October 1979)

After the court appearance Judy was admitted to a detention centre where she underwent the usual testing and fingerprinting. A note was sent to the detention centre advising that 'Judy over the past few months has been increasingly sexually promiscuous' and recommended that 'specific medical examination to exclude disease should be undertaken' (Note on File, 24 October 1979).

Judy had been a victim of incest in both the foster families from which she had tried to escape. Although this fact was known to court officials, the local police and the supervising district officer, after five months in custody Judy was returned to the care of one of these families only to repeat the performance. Early the following year, she was again charged with being uncontrollable and sentenced to an institution (Court Report, 10 January 1980) from which she was released into the care of the same abusive family. When this placement broke down Judy was charged with being destitute and made a ward of the State. She was transferred to a ward hostel from which she absconded many times. During one such escapade, Judy returned to one of the foster homes where she had been abused and administered to herself a near fatal overdose. She was admitted to hospital where she apparently remained in a critical condition for some time (Psychological Assessment for Children's Court, 14 January 1980). Immediately following the suicide attempt, the child welfare authorities charged Judy with absconding from a ward establishment. This is how she came to be committed to an institution for the third and final time during her adolescence.

The sexualisation thesis

Feminist readings of cases like Judy's have tended to direct most of their critique at the role of juvenile justice in punishing sexually active girls. I refer to this reading as 'the sexualisation thesis'. Variations of it have received wide currency in the feminist literature on female delinquency. The following is a brief summary of this literature.

Chesney-Lind's study of sex and juvenile justice in Honolulu Children's Courts in the early 1970s is frequently cited as one of the most significant and original contributions to the sexualisation thesis. This study's major finding claimed that 'the system selects for punishment girls who have transgressed sexually or defied parental authority' (Chesney-Lind, 1974, p. 45). The agencies of juvenile justice were said to sexualise girls' offences in two ways: by punishing girls for sexual misbehaviour and/or by presenting them before the courts on charges of sexual misbehaviour, regardless of their crime (Chesney-Lind, 1974, pp. 45–6). This is said to occur because court officials routinely question girls, not boys, about their sexual behaviour and then use this information to lay additional charges, usually of a status offence nature (Chesney-Lind, 1974, p. 46). Parents, the police and various other court officials are alleged to sexualise girls' offences by translating the crimes of delinquent girls into sexual transgressions. The author of this study takes this as proof that:

> The courts, therefore, often operate under two sets of
> juvenile-delinquency laws, one for boys and one for girls. They
> reserve their harshest and most paternalistic treatment for girls.
> (Chesney-Lind, 1974, p. 42)

Campbell, whose research refers to the American juvenile justice system, also claims that a 'double standard is alive and well. While boys are expected to experiment sexually . . . among girls such behaviour is sufficient grounds for legal action' (Campbell, 1981, p. 8). Shacklady Smith, whose research relates to an English context, concurs that 'offences by girls are sexualised, in fact non-sexual offences are overlooked in favour of sexual (mis)behaviour' (Shacklady Smith, 1978, p. 82). Hancock, whose research on juvenile justice in Victoria has been the most significant to date in the Australian context, claims that her study 'illustrates very clearly the sexualisation of female delinquency and the relative lack of attention to sexual misbehaviour on the part of boys' (Hancock, 1980, p. 10).[4] The editors of the *Australian and New Zealand Journal of Criminology* highlighted the issue in their editorial, suggesting that 'For generations young women have been punished as "delinquents" on grounds of their sexual behaviour' (Broom and Richmond, 1982, p. 66). Summarising from a range of Australian and New Zealand research on female delinquency, Naffine also concluded that 'The agents of the law appear to be preoccupied with the sexuality of girls, while turning a blind eye to the sexual transgressions of boys' (Naffine, 1986, p. 123). Allen has developed a similar line of analysis in her historical account of crimes involving Australian women since 1880. She claims that the history of the criminal justice system is one which has continued to focus on prohibited sexual relationships involving girls under the age of sixteen rather 'than on men's sexual violence or violent sexuality directed at women over sixteen' (Allen, 1990, pp. 241–2). When the criminal justice system has taken action against men for crimes of sexual violence or carnal knowledge Allen argues that the issue has been the girl's morality and not the man's responsibility for the offence (Allen, 1988, pp. 79–80).

Of course there are variations in the arguments presented in these texts. For instance, where Hancock stresses the role of the police in sexualising adolescent female behaviour (Hancock, 1980, p. 9), Shacklady Smith stresses the role of the magistrates and juvenile courts in such processes (Shacklady Smith, 1978, p. 83); while Chesney-Lind (1974) stresses the culpability of the patriarchal family, Allen (1988) stresses the phallocentricism of the justice system. Sometimes, qualifying statements about the relevance of other social factors, such as class, are inserted in arguments about the sexualisation of female delinquency. Hancock, for example, does address the effects of class position on police decisions to either proceed with court action or to issue warnings (Hancock, 1980, p. 10). She argues:

> . . . that those females who are most likely to be affected by a moralistic/welfare definition of the charge and thus presented on a 'protection application', are working-class females whose behaviour is more likely to bring them to police notice, and more likely to contravene dominant and restrictive standards of femininity and morality. (Hancock, 1980, p. 11).

She states that middle-class girls are treated more leniently than working-class girls as a consequence of their being more likely to be defined in legalistic rather than moralistic terms (Hancock, 1980, p. 9).

While more sophisticated than the simplistic notion that juvenile justice operates on two sets of laws, one for boys and one for girls, the analytic framework produced in this feminist discourse becomes a series of equations whereby one essentialism is added to another to consolidate the original gender essentialism (for example, adolescent female + working-class = greater sexualisation). The treatment of working-class girls by the juvenile justice authorities is conceived as an exaggerated version of the kind of sexualisation to which all girls are subject. They are simply 'more likely to contravene dominant and restrictive standards of femininity and morality' (Hancock, 1980, p. 11). Gender essentialism remains intact. The punishment of working-class girls by the Children's Courts becomes a signifier for the sexual regulation of all girls in a patriarchal society. Certainly many more girls from working-class communities appear before the Children's Courts than girls from the more affluent suburbs of Sydney (Table 2.1). Rates of female delinquency in NSW correlate positively with indicators of social disadvantage and negatively with indicators of social advantage.[5] However, it does not necessarily follow that the reason for their over-representation is due to any greater propensity to contravene the restrictive standards of femininity by being more sexually active. The fatal flaw in this argument is that it rests on the bold assumption that working-class girls are indeed more 'sexually promiscuous' than middle-class girls or at least appear to be so to the authorities.

Despite minor variations and qualifications, a remarkably consistent discourse has been reproduced over the last two decades of feminist readings of female delinquency. The justice system has been accused of sexualising the criminal conduct of girls and of punishing the sexual behaviour of girls, while turning a blind eye to the sexual transgressions of boys. Welfare or status complaints have been seen as the vehicle through which sexually active girls have been punished. Delinquent girls are represented in this feminist discourse as doubly punished and twice stigmatised. They are sexual deviants, as well as juvenile delinquents, and nearly always the hapless victims of a double dose of the evils of a justice system which operates 'under two sets of juvenile-delinquency laws, one for boys and one for girls' (Chesney-Lind, 1974, p. 42).

One major problem with this feminist reading, at least in an Australian context, is that the dramatic over-representation of Aboriginal girls and women in the justice system contradicts an insistence on an essential relation between justice and sex. Both this argument and the empirical basis for it are dealt with in the following chapter. I am not suggesting that discourses about

Table 2.1   Detection rates for female delinquency per thousand for metropolitan Sydney [a] [b]

LGA	Detection rate	Female pop. aged 10–19 years	No. of delinquent girls[c]
City	77.4	4779	370
Leichhardt	70.1	3283	230
Liverpool	53.0	9438	500
Marrickville	49.7	6235	310
Concord	45.8	1748	80
Blacktown	38.9	18506	720
Bankstown	37.3	12611	470
Botany	33.2	2708	90
Holroyd	32.9	7000	230
Waverley	31.9	3757	120
Auburn	31.3	3519	110
Burwood	31.1	2248	70
Campbelltown	28.6	8038	230
Gosford	27.2	6620	180
Fairfield	24.9	12130	300
Hurstville	24.9	5213	130
Penrith	24.7	9312	230
North Sydney	24.2	2066	50
Wyong	24.1	4569	110
Rockdale	21.2	5660	120
Strathfield	20.2	1979	40
Sutherland	19.8	14175	280
Drummoyne	19.7	2026	40
Camden	19.7	1526	30
Hawkesbury	19.6	3057	60
Blue Mountains	19.2	4160	80
Hornsby	17.8	10125	180
Ashfield	17.6	2849	50
Randwick	17.6	7949	140
Manly	17.4	2305	40
Canterbury	17.3	9833	170
Kogarah	17.1	3501	60
Woollahra	15.4	3233	50
Lane Cove	15.3	1952	30
Hunters Hill	13.0	771	10
Parramatta	12.8	10911	140
Baulkham Hills	11.9	9211	110
Warringah	11.0	14562	160
Ryde	9.1	6568	60
Willoughby	8.3	3606	30
Ku-ring-gai	4.9	10163	50
Mosman	0.0	1623	0

Notes: [a] Population data based on 1981 census as this time period falls within that which most of the girls in the study were appearing before the NSW Children's Courts.

[b] 1638 girls aged 10–19 years from Wollondilly LGA have been excluded due to coding difficulty.

[c] Born in years 1960–1964.

sexuality are not authoritative in contexts where court action is taken against Aboriginal girls or women. Clearly, sometimes it is (see Chapter 2 and Goodall, 1990, pp. 6–9). Nor am I suggesting that there is an essential relation between race and criminal justice which simply displaces an essential relation between criminal justice and gender. What I am arguing is that despite the glaring historical relevance that colonialist discourses have had on shaping the administration of justice in Australia, this relevance has been curiously absent in feminist readings of female crime and delinquency. The 'Australian women' in Allen's book, for example, are all white, yet Aboriginal women have been and continue to be incarcerated at a rate higher than Aboriginal men and demonstrably higher than non-Aboriginal women. Some would see this omission as exemplary of the exclusion of black women's perspectives from Eurocentric feminist perspectives more generally (Amos and Parmar, 1984; Carby, 1982; Gunew, 1991; Hooks, 1984).

Even where concerns about the specificity of black women have been considered in feminist discourses the issue has tended to be dealt with by simply adding one essentialism onto another, that is: racism + sexism = black women = white women only more so (Harris, 1990). Any discursive framework which is essentialist (and it does not have to be feminist to be essentialist, see glossary) is incapable of considering the multiplicity of discourses which operate in the administration of juvenile justice in a given context. For example, even if arguments about the sexualisation thesis were to incorporate concerns about race (as they have about class), Aboriginal girls could only be constructed in this discursive framework as the bearers of a multiple oppression. Aboriginal girls can only be represented in this discourse as the subjects of a more intense form of sexualisation by the agencies of justice (that is, adolescent female + Aboriginality = greater sexualisation = white girls only more so). Clearly, such an argument is deficient. The specificity of Aboriginal girls gets lost in the category of female delinquency. Concerns about the fundamentally different ways in which Aboriginal girls have been historically processed by the juvenile justice and child welfare authorities are submerged while concerns about the centrality of sex are curiously strengthened! As a way of avoiding this mistake the following chapter has been devoted to investigating the specificity of the processing of Aboriginal girls by the justice authorities.

Despite these conceptual weaknesses, the sexualisation thesis seems to have considerable empirical support in the form of sex differences recorded in juvenile crime statistics. An assessment of these particular feminist readings of sex and statistics follows.

Sex and statistics

Almost all publications which address the issue of female delinquency—feminist, non-feminist or otherwise—are prefaced by the
argument that delinquent girls are numerically insignificant in comparison with delinquent boys. It is also commonly observed that
most girls appear in court for non-criminal charges, variously
referred to as 'status', 'welfare' or 'care and protection' complaints,
whereas most boys appear on charges of criminal behaviour (Hancock and Chesney-Lind, 1982, p. 109). It is also often alleged that
girls are treated more harshly before the courts than boys (Hampton,
1979, p. 24; Campbell, 1981, p. 203; Shacklady Smith, 1978, p.
74). I will deal with these three empirical claims separately.

The proposition that boys far outnumber girls in recorded rates
of juvenile court statistics is indisputable and clearly depicted in
official rates in NSW Children's Court Statistics (Fig. 2.1).[6] Since
1960 the sex differential has fluctuated between four to six boys
for every girl appearing before the State Children's Courts. This sex
ratio is similar for other Australian States. In South Australia, boys
are convicted four times as often as girls (Omedei, 1979, p. 83). In
Queensland, five and a half times as many boys appeared before
the courts as girls (Fielding, 1977, p. 173). The numerical
predominance of boys in juvenile court statistics seems to be an
internationally based empirical phenomenon. In the United States,
the arrest ratio of boys to girls is approximately four to one (Sarri,
1974, p. 67). In Scotland, six boys appear before the courts for
every girl (May, 1977, p. 205). Chesney-Lind's (1977) study of sex
differentials in rates of offending for Honolulu reports a similar
variation in the ratio of boys to girls. I have no dispute with these
findings. In 1956, Cohen made the observation that 'Practically all
published figures . . . agree, . . . male delinquency is at least four
times as common as female delinquency' (Cohen, 1956, p. 45). This
however is where the agreement ends.

The second statistical 'fact' invoked as proof of a sexualisation
process is that girls are over-represented in welfare matters
compared to boys, or that more girls than boys appear before the
courts for such matters. Chesney-Lind's study, for example, reported
that 70 per cent of all girls brought before a Honolulu juvenile court
appeared on status complaints compared with 31 per cent of all boys
(Chesney-Lind, 1974, p. 45). Australian studies have published
similar findings. Hancock, for example, claims that the majority of
girls (63 per cent) before the courts in Victoria appeared on care
and protection matters and that boys were least likely to appear on
protection applications (8 per cent), and most often appeared for
property-related offences (56 per cent) (Hancock and Chesney-Lind,

**Figure 2.1   Total court appearances by sex, NSW Children's Courts
1960–90**

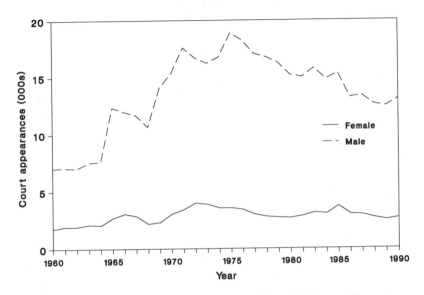

Source: YACS Annual Reports 1960–83, NSW Bureau of Crime Statistics and Research
1984–90.

1982, p. 112). Fielding drew a similar comparison between girls and
boys using official statistics for Queensland. Her study concludes
that 7 per cent of males compared to 42 per cent of females before
the Children's Courts in that State appeared under 'care, protection
and control' matters, while the remaining 58 per cent of girls and
93 per cent of boys appeared for criminal offences (Fielding, 1977,
pp. 173–6). On the basis of these comparisons the conclusion is
usually drawn that girls are therefore demonstrably over-represented
before the courts in status, welfare or non-criminal matters in
relation to boys. It is then commonly inferred that most girls before
the courts are being punished for sexual (mis)behaviour, for which
boys are not. There are several difficulties with this interpretation
of sex and statistics.

   Not only has the empirical basis of this claim eroded since the
initial publication of this particular feminist reading of juvenile
crime statistics (Fig. 2.2), but the empirical basis was not even
strong in Australia at the time (from 1974 onwards) the sexualisation
thesis assumed currency among Australian authors. Welfare
complaints have been fairly evenly distributed between the sexes in
the States of Queensland, New South Wales, Western Australia,

Figure 2.2 Offending profile of girls before NSW Children's Courts 1960–90

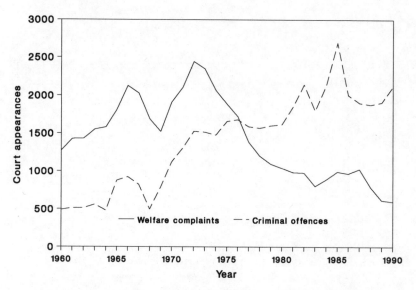

Source: YACS Annual Reports 1960–83, NSW Bureau of Crime Statistics and Research 1984–90.

South Australia and Victoria since about the mid-1970s. This trend is clearly depicted in Figure 2.3. The pattern has even reversed in New South Wales since 1976 with the majority of girls now appearing before the courts for criminal offences and not for welfare complaints (Fig. 2.2).

My second difficulty with the claim that girls are more likely to appear before the courts on welfare matters than boys lies in the way in which findings are represented in those studies which purport to prove this: they all use, for the purposes of statistical comparison, a percentage breakdown of the numbers of adolescents appearing for welfare and criminal matters by sex. For example, using figures for New South Wales (NSW), the comparison could be drawn that, since 1960, an average of 9 per cent of court appearances involving boys were for welfare complaints whereas this figure for girls was an average of 54 per cent. Also, that 91 per cent of the court appearances relating to boys involved criminal offences compared with an average of 46 per cent for girls (Table 2.2 and Fig. 2.2). An alternative, more rigorous method of comparing rates per head of the male and female adolescent populations which is used in the analysis of crime statistics (see, for example, Freiberg, *et al.*, 1988,

Figure 2.3 Interstate comparison of sex differences in welfare/criminal offences

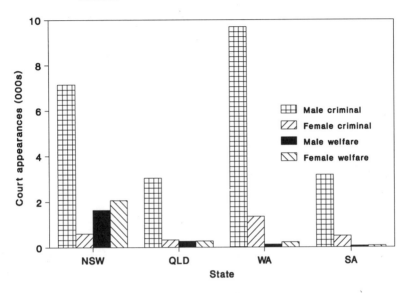

Source: 1974 Annual Reports for respective State Departments.

p. 35) has not been used to empirically substantiate the claim that more girls than boys appear before the courts for welfare complaints. Using statistics for New South Wales, and assuming that the adolescent population is equally divided between male and female, this method indicates that almost *equal* proportions of the adolescent male and female populations have appeared before the courts for welfare matters since the mid-1970s (Fig. 2.4). Strictly speaking, it is therefore misleading to state that, 'females are much more likely than males to be presented to court on status offence grounds' (Hancock and Chesney-Lind, 1985, p. 237) because when taken as proportions of their *respective* adolescent populations, as many boys as girls are presented to court for welfare matters. This has been so in most Australian States since the mid-1970s when the sexualisation thesis first gained currency in the Australian literature.

I am not suggesting that numerical parity indicates the absence of sexual difference in the way welfare complaints are administered, but I am suggesting that in statistical terms, the most significant sex differential relates not to *welfare* matters, but to *criminal* matters. The adolescent female population has been and continues to be massively under-represented in criminal matters before the NSW Children's Courts compared with the adolescent male

Table 2.2   Offending profile of boys before the NSW Children's Courts

Year	Welfare matters	%	Criminal offences	%	Total
1960	927	13	6128	87	7055
1961	979	14	6090	86	7069
1962	1129	16	5899	84	7028
1963	1157	15	6394	85	7551
1964	1161	15	6473	85	7634
1965	1136	9	11220	91	12356
1966	1390	12	10588	88	11978
1967	1300	11	10387	89	11687
1968	1148	11	9502	89	10650
1969	1271	9	12822	91	14093
1970	1482	10	13863	90	15345
1971	1384	8	16202	92	16710
1972	1552	9	15158	91	16710
1973	1488	9	14726	91	16214
1974	1641	10	15111	90	16752
1975	1445	8	17400	92	18845
1976	1310	7	16938	93	18248
1977	1085	6	15960	94	17045
1978	1110	7	15644	93	16754
1979	1080	7	15174	93	16254
1980	975	6	14227	94	15202
1981	976	7	14025	93	15001
1982	959	6	14809	94	15768
1983	1004	9	10694	91	11698
1984	912	6	13905	94	14817
1985	923	6	14411	94	15334
1986	875	7	12355	93	13230
1987	853	6	12542	94	13395
1988	704	6	11910	94	12614
1989	533	4	12316	96	12849
1990	620	5	12540	95	13160

Notes: Data for criminal offences by sex only available for proven matters for 1983
         and from 1988 onwards and for welfare matters in 1983.
Source: YACS Annual Reports 1960–83, NSW Bureau Crime Statistics and Research
         1984–90.

population (Fig. 2.5). The offence profiles by sex represented in
Figure 2.6 summarise this dynamic. On the basis of these figures,
one could forcefully argue that here is an example of the way in
which feminist criminology has failed in its attempts to make
criminology confront its question of sex in relation to the male sex
(Allen, 1989, p. 23). The masculinity of criminality, rather than the
sexualisation of female delinquency, is the question to be addressed
here. While this is not the aim of this book such a project has been
a welcome preoccupation of others (Allen, 1989; White, 1990;
Cunneen, 1985, p. 85).

My third difficulty with the empirical basis of the sexualisation

Figure 2.4 Welfare matters by sex, NSW Childrens Courts 1960–90

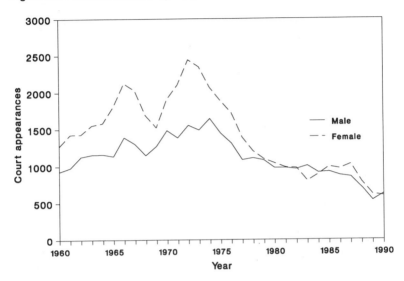

Source: YACS Annual Reports 1960–83, NSW Bureau Crime Statistics and Research
1984–90.

Figure 2.5 Criminal offences by sex, NSW Children's Courts 1960–90

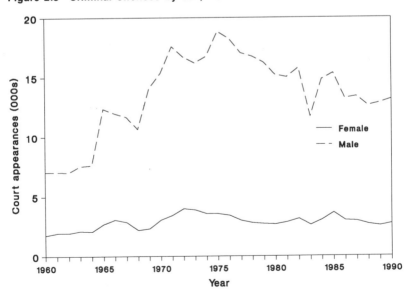

Source: YACS Annual Reports 1960–83, NSW Bureau Crime Statistics and Research
1984–90.

Figure 2.6   Offence profiles by sex, NSW Children's Courts 1960–90

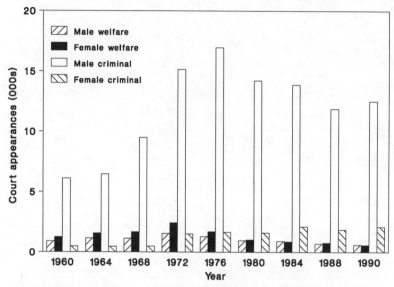

Source: YACS Annual Reports 1960–83, NSW Bureau Crime Statistics and Research 1984–90.

thesis concerns the certainty with which legal categories have been interpreted to suggest that girls are being dragged before the courts for sexual misbehaviour. It is too confidently assumed that girls brought before the courts for welfare matters are actually before the courts for sexual misconduct (see, for example, Fielding, 1977, p. 176; Hancock, 1980, p. 7). But even where this is the case, as it was in Judy's, reasons for court action are not easily reducible to a singular relationship between sex and justice. Children's Court statistics are the products of a complex criminalisation process. Like other official statistics they are not neutral records but social products mediated by work practices, organisational factors, and the conceptual and technical instruments of classification (Miles and Irvine, 1979, p.124). The content of female delinquency cannot be read off from statistical aggregates of Children's Court statistics. To do so entails the reification of legal categories as vague and indiscriminate as 'being uncontrollable', 'neglected' or 'exposed to moral danger' under which a diverse range of behaviours can be brought before the court. It is simply far too problematic to assume with any confidence, as the sexualisation thesis does, that welfare complaints arise from allegations about sexual misconduct.[7] Subsequent chapters in this book explore the many factors and contexts in which welfare complaints have been laid against particular girls. Sexual conduct is certainly one of these factors, but it is not necessarily the only or deciding one.

The third empirical claim generally invoked as proof of a sexualisation process is that girls are punished by the courts more severely than boys. This is a claim which appears to have considerable empirical substance (Campbell, 1981, pp. 203–7; Chesney-Lind, 1974, p. 45; Hampton, 1979, p. 29; Hancock and Chesney-Lind, 1982, p. 109 and 1985, p. 236; Hancock, 1980, p. 10; Shacklady Smith, 1978, p. 82; Terry, 1970, p. 86). On the basis of these studies girls are said to be more likely to receive supervisory orders and custodial sentences than boys.

Few of these studies involve a control for offence categories but when court orders are analysed in relation to offence profiles a more complex picture emerges. New South Wales statistics for 1979 have been used for the purposes of illustrating the argument (Table 2.3). They are not atypical, they fall within the period under review and they depict the *same* kinds of patterns identified by most other comparable studies. Of the girls before the courts for welfare matters, 16 per cent were committed to institutions compared with only 5 per cent of those appearing for criminal matters. In the same year, 21 per cent of boys appearing for welfare matters were committed to corrective institutions, whereas only 10 per cent of boys appearing on criminal charges were committed. Proportionally, more of the girls (31 per cent) before the courts on criminal charges were admonished and discharged than those (20 per cent) who appeared in court on welfare complaints. Similarly for the boys (21 per cent and 16 per cent respectively). Hence penalties were severe for *both* cohorts of girls and boys who appeared before the courts on welfare matters. What is significant here is not so much the sex of the child but the *means by which they ended up before the court* as being a welfare case and not a criminal case.

Even when offence profiles are discarded, the result is still ambiguous because girls who appear before the courts are treated more leniently in some ways than in others. When both welfare and criminal matters are taken into consideration almost equal proportions of girls and boys were committed to institutions—at 9 per cent and 10 per cent of their respective populations appearing before the courts. To be admonished and discharged is to receive one of the most lenient penalties available to the Children's Court. In both welfare and criminal categories, as well as in terms of total matters, more girls than boys received this order. Fines and probation orders are notable exceptions to this pattern. Higher percentages of girls were released on probation and considerably more boys than girls were fined.

**Table 2.3 Penalty by sex for welfare and criminal matters, NSW
Children's Courts, 1979**

Penalty	Girls		Boys	
	no.	(%)	no	(%)
Committed to wardship[b]				
welfare matters	288	26	335	31
criminal offences	4	0[a]	58	0[a]
sub-total	292	11	393	3
Committed to institution[c]				
welfare matters	172	16	229	21
criminal offences	79	5	1463	10
sub-total	251	9	1692	10
Released on probation				
welfare matters	405	37	320	30
criminal offences	467	29	3183	21
sub-total	872	32	3503	22
Admonished & discharged				
welfare matters	217	20	174	16
criminal offences	492	31	3112	21
sub-total	709	26	3286	20
Fined				
welfare matters	1	0[a]	1	0[a]
criminal offences	543	34	7176	47
sub-total	544	20	7177	44
Other court orders				
welfare matters	14	1	21	2
criminal offences	14	1	182	1
sub-total	28	1	203	1
Total welfare	1097	100	1080	100
Total criminal	1599	100	15174	100
Total court orders	2696	100	16254	100

Notes: [a] Rounding error.
           [b] Includes committal to care of approved person.
           [c] Includes suspended committals.
Source: YACS Annual Report 1979, p. 147.

The argument that girls are treated more harshly than their male
counterparts who appear before the Children's Courts has to
confront a number of complexities. On the one hand, girls before
the courts could be said to be treated more leniently than boys
because they are more often admonished and less often committed
to institutions. On the other hand, girls before the courts could be
said to be treated more severely than boys because they are more
often released on probation and less often fined. Some of the studies

quoted above do acknowledge this ambiguity. Hancock's study, for example, does recognise that girls presented on 'protection applications' are dealt with more severely than girls whose behaviour is interpreted in legalistic terms (Hancock, 1980, p. 10). This study also recognises that girls appearing before the courts on criminal charges are, in some respects, dealt with more leniently than boys (Hancock, 1980, p. 9) and also that recommendations for institutionalisation are roughly equal for both sexes (Hancock, 1980, p. 10).

To ask the question, why is it that welfare cases are treated more harshly than criminal cases whilst important, seems to have been overlooked in feminist readings of sex and statistics. One particular finding from my own statistical analysis of the offending profile of the 1046 girls is relevant here. Before reaching eighteen years of age the 1046 girls in the sample had 2046 court appearances among them recorded against their names in the JCI. Although their offence profiles were almost equally divided between criminal matters and welfare complaints, when these *same* girls appeared before the courts for welfare matters they were much more likely to be committed to an institution (see Table 7.1, Chapter 7). There is little support here for the argument that working-class girls tend to be processed more frequently as welfare cases while middle-class girls are classified as criminal offenders. It is the same girls, most of whom are from socially disadvantaged backgrounds (Table 2.1), who are being punished by the courts more severely when they present as welfare cases rather than criminal cases. As stated above, the issue here is not so much the sex of the child, although it can be important, but rather the nexus that exists between welfare and punishment. Chapter 7 deals specifically with this important issue, and each of the following chapters contribute in some way to the development of this argument.

One possible explanation for the nexus between welfare and punishment which is explored in subsequent chapters is that the disposition of both girls and boys before the courts for welfare matters is guided by the expertise of social work and psychological discourses. This means that the penalties imposed by the Children's Court in relation to welfare matters are not shaped by the judicial logic of the penalty tariff but by the logic of social work and psychology. Because these discourses advocate earlier intervention and longer periods of supervision and institutionalisation, such as taking 'children at risk' into custody or placing them under supervision *before* they commit criminal offences, the disposition of welfare cases (for both males and females) comes under a grid of calculations which are more interventionist, and experienced as more punitive, than the disposition of criminal cases by the Children's Courts.

Feminist readings of female delinquency

Feminist readings of female delinquency have tended not only to overstate the centrality of discourses authorised around sex but in so doing have also actually *misread* their effects. By positing the effectivity of discourses about sex in some sovereign form of patriarchal power which operates from the outside upon the field of juvenile justice and its specific mechanisms for processing delinquent girls, the opportunity to analyse their production within this particular site of government is foregone. In order to illustrate this, what follows is a juxtaposition of two possible readings of Judy's notes. Her case was chosen from other available possibilities[8] precisely because it fitted, more neatly than others, the basic propositions of the sexualisation thesis. In other words, Judy's case is nowhere near as ambiguous as others in the sample. Ostensibly her sexual conduct seemed to be the most important reason for the court action taken against her.

Reading one

Judy's case notes describe her as a sexually active girl. On every occasion she appeared before the courts she was punished by the Children's Courts for sexual conduct which transgressed double standards of morality. Her case notes documented many examples where this occurred. After questioning Judy at length about her sexual conduct, the district officer, for example, then used this information to charge her with breaching the terms of her probation. During the court proceedings a great deal of information about Judy's sexuality was presented to the court as evidence in the case against her. The court was informed that Judy was promiscuous and deliberately amoral, boasting freely about her sexual relations with boys (Court Report, 10 August 1979). She was accused of seeking sexual relations with boys for instrumental rather than romantic reasons. She was also accused of 'using sex as a means for boosting her self-esteem' (Psychological Assessment, 14 January 1981) and not as a path to marriage, monogamy or motherhood. She was regarded as selfish and unnatural because she sought pleasure through sex. Judy's institutionalisation seemed motivated by a desire to control and punish her promiscuous behaviour (Home Report, 24 April 1980). In one Court Report it was even suggested that she be locked up for her own protection (Court Report, 20 October 1979).

Discourses about sexuality which make women the moral

guardians of a naturally uncontrollable male sexuality, shaped the official response to Judy in two main ways. First, in relation to the incident on the school bus where Judy was pressed into undoing her blouse, it was her sexuality and not that of the boys which was considered central to the incident. By being represented as an evil seductress and a temptation to naturally playful young boys, Judy was made responsible for the sexist behaviour of the boys on that bus. Second, in relation to Judy's experience of incest, it was her sexuality and not that of the three men in two different foster families who sexually abused her over a period of about eight years which was scrutinised, moralised and subject to court action. She was the one held responsible for the intrafamilial sexuality in which she was a relatively defenceless party. In this context, the argument that the justice authorities turn a blind eye to the transgressions of male sexuality while preoccupying themselves with the normative transgressions of female sexuality appears to be a forceful account of what happened to Judy. It could then be inferred that court action against girls like Judy is no more than a patriarchal form of social control which seeks to police double standards of sexuality, exempting boys from any such repression.

Reading two

Certainly Judy's sexuality was the object of a great deal of punitive and moralistic juvenile justice intervention. But the discourses which sought to punish and normalise her conduct, including her sexuality, cannot be reduced to the solitary effect of one underlying form of masculinist power. A multitude of discourses entered into the disciplining of her body and her formation as a delinquent girl. Departmental personnel vested with the responsibility for supervising Judy thought that she 'lacked constructive leisure and social activities' (Psychological Assessment, 17 January 1981), needed to establish 'organised social and leisure activities' (Psychological Assessment, 17 January 1981) and be 'introduced to a more socially acceptable peer group' (Social Work Report on Institution Inmate, 26 March 1981) in order to 'lessen the extent of her undesirable peer dependence' (Social Work Report on Institution Inmate, 26 March 1981). Her sexuality was represented in these documents as an integral part of an undesirable cultural context and peer group set, for example:

> She is only fifteen and a half years old, associates with the least desirable local youth and I do not feel that she has progressed greatly in learning to control her impulsive promiscuous behaviour. I fear that it will not be long before she is again before the Court.
> (Home Report, 24 April 1980)

Judy's sexual promiscuity did not singularly provide the motivation for court action against her. Rather it was the way in which she negotiated her sexuality so visibly within a particular cultural context and then defied attempts to restrict and normalise her conduct which signalled so much danger to the juvenile justice authorities. Her body invaded and sought sexual pleasure in the public arena with youths (both male and female) regarded as 'undesirable' others by the authorities. Her body also emitted signs of danger in physical maturity, sexual vulnerability and 'cheap' appearance. She sported tattoos, wore jeans and thongs and pink mid-drift tops (Description of New Admission, 31 January 1980). Her body was described as 'physically mature—looking much older than her years would suggest' (Note on File, undated). Her behaviour disrupted not only norms about female sexuality, femininity and romance but norms about adolescence as an extended period of childhood. Because her body looked much older than her years suggest it was seen by the authorities as a trap to the unwary male unable to control the solicitations of such a 'brazen young hussy'.[9] Similar comments were made in many of the cases I examined. Anny Johns, for example, was described as 'a mature pleasant lass who responded cautiously when seen' and whose 'current trouble seemed to result from her impulsiveness and failure to control herself around boys' (Psychological Report, 3 November 1977). The medical officer who examined Anny in the remand shelter wrote in his report that the 'girl has had considerable sexual experience and easily admits three fingers'. This information was then forwarded on with other court documents to be considered by the magistrate in sentencing Anny.

There is no doubt as to the justice authorities' intense and moralistic concern with the sexual conduct of both these girls. However to see this concern simply as a form of social control which only seeks to repress adolescent *female* sexuality is to miss the crucial point that the regulation of socially injurious forms of *male* sexuality, such as incest, rape and carnal knowledge, also operate through technologies of government centred on the corporeality of young women. Let me explain how. Because male sexuality is understood in masculinist discourses as being instinctive, male sexual urges are regarded as being biologically driven. Hence it is incumbent on females to govern their bodies and conduct in such a way as to not arouse the instinctive sex-striving of the male sex (Tyler, 1986, pp. 55–58). This means that the only strategic mechanisms of governance conceivable for dealing with undesirable forms of male sexuality actually operate through the bodies of the female sex. While the effect of these technologies of government may limit and order the corporeal positions legitimately available to girls, they are primarily intended to control male sexual deviance through the prevention of arousal. Of course, this is all dreadfully misguided and repressive for girls but, it also has repressive effects on undesirable forms of *male* sexuality, such as incest and rape, which, in vital respects, disrupt discourses about family life, manhood and nationhood. The problem is that girls are made responsible for ensuring that they do not fall prey to undesirable forms of male sexuality. In other words, it is their social duty to be sexually coy and it is incumbent on mothers to instruct their daughters on how to discipline their bodies in such techniques of the self (Tyler, 1986).

Here is where Judy went 'wrong'. By failing to discipline the sexual imagery of her body in the habit of sexual coyness she refused to take responsibility for controlling male sexuality. In other words, she refused to fulfil her civic duty to police male sexuality and in so doing was seen as having set herself up as the victim of deviant male sexual impulses commonly understood as 'uncontrollable'. The fact that she was sexually harassed on the school bus, continually taken advantage of by adolescent boys, and raped by three men in her foster family was taken by the authorities as evidence of Judy's unwillingness to police the undesirable solicitations of sexually devious men. The juvenile justice authorities could then rationalise Judy's punishment as a form of benevolence. They say her periods of incarceration were not intended to punish her but, rather, to protect her from the designing men from whom she could not protect herself! Here we see most clearly the overlapping of discourses about sexuality and benevolence which have the effect of enmeshing welfare with punishment and care with control. The discourses of blame are inverted. Judy is no longer the victim of sexual molestation. Her 'innocence' is lost through being sexually abused and so, through no fault of her own, she becomes subsumed into the discourses about 'uncontrollable girls' and subject to their concomitant forms of discipline.

The hysterical fears about Judy's body and behaviour were not just confined to fears about her loss of 'sexual innocence'. Judy is not atypical of the youth who are routinely processed through the juvenile justice system. She comes from humble origins; had rebelled against the requirements of the school system at an early age; participated in a youth culture centred around visible street activities which defied the dominant norms of family life and leisure consumption; and, when confronted with attempts to correct her ways by welfare officials, school counsellors and the courts, she rejected these as well. She was defiant, she took little notice of court orders refusing to accept the supervision of the district officer,

she resented 'limits on her freedom' imposed by Orders of the Court
and she had a 'bad attitude' to figures of authority (particularly the
district officer and the school counsellor). One supervising district
officer described Judy's attitude in the following terms.

> Judy does not wish any involvement with 'The Welfare'. She
> perceives us as the enemy. (Annual Report on Ward, 20 February
> 1982)

In all the court actions taken against Judy, considerations about
her guilt or innocence and about the severity or otherwise of the
offences she committed were subordinated to a series of assessments
about which one of the available sentencing options was, in the
view of the experts (the psychologist and the district officer), the
most appropriate given Judy's failure to fulfil her social duty to
ensure her own protection. The psychologist, for example, prepared
the Court Report after Judy's attempted suicide and interpreted the
suicide attempt as evidence of an inability to cope in the community.
In lieu of this, the psychologist suggested it was therefore appropriate for the court to commit her to a secure institution. This section
of the Psychological Assessment for the Children's Court read as
follows:

> When seen Judy was not depressed, but it was obvious she is unable
> to cope within the community at this stage. However, her
> self-esteem is low. She is sexually promiscuous, using sex as a
> means of boosting her self-esteem . . . It would probably be best for
> Judy to go to a training school for a couple of months and then
> perhaps [be] returned to a ward establishment for the last month or
> so of her committal. Attempts could then be made to find her
> employment, even if it was voluntary work. *Recommendation*:
> Committal to an Institution (Court Report, 14 January 1981)

The basis of her incarceration is quite transparent: not the commission of any legal offence, but the repeated and escalated transgression of infra-legal norms of adolescence, schooling, sexuality,
leisure and family life. Girls like Judy pass into the hands of district
officers, police and the courts and their auxiliary forms of expertise
(psychology and social work) through need, vulnerability or dependency on welfare. This is how the justice authorities acquired the
means through which Judy's sexuality and conduct at school, on the
bus and in the streets could be scrutinised and subjected to court
action. Judy was desperate for the kind of housing and emotional
and material support young people ordinarily acquire through their
attachment to families. Through absolutely no fault of her own she
did not have a family and the one to which she was artificially
attached sexually and emotionally abused her. Clearly she needed

assistance to escape an abusive foster family, but securing it meant subjecting herself to the disciplinary processes of State 'care' (Carlen, 1987). Once in State care Judy was then driven along the 'fast track' from care to detention, as is the fate of so many State wards.

Comparison of readings one and two

In the first reading of Judy's notes I isolated gender and conceived the primary function of juvenile justice intervention with girls to be the policing of adolescent female sexuality. In the second reading, I attempted to analyse the function of juvenile justice intervention in terms of the discourses of sexuality, benevolence and 'problem children' which have become integral to the administration of present day juvenile justice. In the first reading I sought to essentialise the relation between sex and justice as something pre-existing acting from the outside in. In the second reading I sought to de-essentialise that relation by locating the power effects of masculinist discourses in their conditions of internal production within the forms of government set up to manage 'offending' girls. I am not suggesting that there are only two possible feminist readings. Obviously, Judy's notes are open to multiple readings. But I am suggesting that the second reading is more convincing for the following reasons.

In essentialist feminist readings the patriarchal family, father or judge has been identified as the vehicle through which girls' offences are sexualised. Those who initiated the court action against Judy, and against most of the girls who appear before the Children's Courts in NSW, fit neither of these descriptions. They are the 'experts'—social workers, district officers, school counsellors and psychologists—and most of them are women. So, the sexualising process, to the extent that there is one, has, for the most part of this century, primarily operated among women—including mothers, their daughters, female social workers and police officers. Indeed, women were initially recruited into the NSW Police Force for the sole purpose of dealing with adult and juvenile female offenders (Cunneen in Findlay and Hogg, 1988, p. 193). It has been too confidently assumed in essentialist readings of female delinquency that the vehicle of sexualisation is some patriarchal family or some male magistrate, father or police officer, rather than some female social worker, district officer, school counsellor or departmental psychologist. The second reading of Judy's notes avoids this closure. It does not seek to pin down the locus of power to any one particular sovereign source or patriarchal figure or vehicle. Rather, it seeks to analyse how a multiplicity of discourses overlap in the processing of girls by the juvenile justice system which produces as one of its effects the punishment of girls considered to have 'lost' their 'sexual innocence'.

The effects of masculinist discourses are open to greater scrutiny when examined in terms of their internal production within specific sites of governance. This is what the second reading of Judy's notes attempts to do and the first does not. In the second reading I analysed how masculinist discourses about sexuality produce their effects through governmental technologies which operate upon the bodies of girls. In this reading the power of masculinist discourses about female sexuality was located, not so much in a sexualisation process (where an essentialist reading would locate it) but in an alliance between welfare and judicial prescriptions for modern juvenile justice intervention. This alliance has not only made the female body the site of government for undesirable forms of male sexuality, such as incest and carnal knowledge, but it has also created an infra-legal context in which masculinist discourses about the failure of girls to police undesirable forms of male sexuality can authorise punitive measures of juvenile justice intervention. Such an overlap has also generated a mechanism for punishing girls who fail to fulfil their social duty of taking responsibility for the control of male sexuality through coyness and other forms of discipline of the body. Hence we see the criss-crossing of benevolent discourses with masculinist ones and their mutual institution in technologies for governing adolescent girls.

The dispersion of judicial power to the experts that has occurred during this century has multiplied the sites and means for normalising all kinds of conduct including sexual conduct regarded as being inappropriate for adolescents. Essentialist readings about sex and justice by concentrating on establishing the pre-existence of a systematic sexualisation process have not looked at how the internal production of discourses within juvenile justice administration work through and have as their point of application the bodies of adolescent girls.

Summary

In this chapter I have attempted to clear the ground for the development of a different kind of feminist reading of female delinquency. At an empirical level I have taken issue with the statistical foundations supporting the sexualisation thesis and concluded that they ought not to be privileged as representing the only possible feminist reading of sex and statistics. Girls are not necessarily dealt with more harshly than boys and girls are *not* over-represented in statistics for welfare matters in most Australian

States. The fact that boys far outnumber girls brought before the courts is the only indisputable empirical claim of the sexualisation thesis, at least in the Australian context. The most important statistical sex differential, that boys are involved in much higher levels of criminality than girls, has been left untheorised in feminist readings of sex and juvenile court statistics, as it has been in most mainstream criminology (Allen, 1988). The issue here is the masculinity of criminality not the sexualisation of female delinquency. The other really important statistical pattern, that both girls and boys appearing before the courts as welfare cases are more harshly treated than those appearing for criminal offences, has either been inadequately addressed or misconstrued as evidence that girls are more harshly treated by the courts than boys. Again, the issue here is not the sexualisation of female delinquency but the blurring of care with control, of welfare with justice, and the inversion of discourses of blame which make the victim (in this case the abused child) the guilty party.

The crux of my argument in this chapter has taken issue with essentialist concepts, such as patriarchy, and their relevance in understanding the operation of juvenile justice. By assuming that the justice system punishes sexually active girls in its service to maintaining patriarchy, the sexualisation thesis constructs a fictive account of a complex criminalisation process and produces an array of unhelpful and unnecessary closures. Even where sexual misconduct is the primary concern of juvenile justice intervention, as it was in Judy's case, essentialist readings have misunderstood how masculinist discourses operate through such mechanisms. Delinquent girls are not a homogeneous group—they are differentiated in relation to the operation of juvenile justice. Essentialist positions on this issue are fundamentally misdirected (Carlen, 1988).

The concern of the juvenile justice authorities just with the regulation of adolescent female sexuality has been vastly overstated in essentialist readings of female delinquency. Not only is the burden of this regulation spread unevenly throughout the adolescent female population, but the object of this regulation may in fact be undesirable forms of male sexuality. The strategic point for feminist intervention, as I see it, is to suggest how abusive and violent forms of male sexuality, such as incest, can be governed in ways other than through the discipline of the adolescent female body as it was in Judy's case.

3 Aboriginal girls and juvenile justice

The extraordinary level of Aboriginal criminalisation in Australia is usually seen as the result either of over-policing or over-offending or even as a combination of both these. An essentialism which reduces the actual and diverse workings of a range of justice and welfare institutions to the single effect of racism can be detected in these accounts. Certainly, Aboriginal girls are vastly and consistently over-represented at every level of the juvenile justice system in every State of Australia. While this extraordinary level of over-representation contradicts an essentialised relation between sex and justice, it does not necessarily flow from this that there is an essentialised relation between race and justice. While race has been disavowed as a legitimate grounds for welfare intervention since the abolition of the Aborigines Welfare Board in 1969, the argument developed in this chapter seeks to show how discourses about child welfare, health and psychology in particular, have continued to have a profound criminalising impact on marginal populations, and on Aboriginal girls in particular. The argument divides into two parts. The first presents a summary of the empirical research which documents the rate of Aboriginal criminalisation in various State jurisdictions. The second and more substantive section of the chapter attempts to analyse the specific ways in which Aboriginal girls have been drawn into the juvenile justice system in the State of New South Wales.

Levels of over-representation

Empirical evidence of this over-representation of Aboriginal girls, and youth and adults more generally, in the juvenile justice and adult criminal justice systems in Australian States, is overwhelming. In my statistical analysis of the criminal records of 1046 delinquent girls the most over-represented cohort came from rural Aboriginal communities (r=.61) (Table 3.1). When these rates were broken down into smaller regions, the level of over-representation increased dramatically for five of these localities, namely Bourke, Walgett, Brewarrina, Wilcannia and Moree (Table 3.2), where Aboriginal populations vastly exceed the NSW State average. The rate of female delinquency in these regions was four times the average for rural NSW and three times the average for metropolitan Sydney.

Other NSW studies have also documented vast discrepancies between the proportions of Aboriginal and non-Aboriginal youth drawn into the justice system. One limitation with this body of research is that the specificity of Aboriginal girls has been lost within the more general category 'Aboriginal youth' but there is no other comparable data which controls for sex. Cunneen and Robb's study of criminal justice in north-west NSW calculated that:

> . . . the charge rates for Aboriginal youth are six times greater in Dubbo, forty-seven times greater in Wellington, fifty-seven times greater in Brewarrina, thirty-six times greater in Bourke and ninety

Table 3.1 Detection rates for female delinquency per thousand population in rural NSW

Rural statistical division[a]	Detection rate	Female population aged 10–19 years	Per cent population Aboriginal	No. of delinqent girls[c]
Far-west	46.5	2578	2.7	120
North-west	35.9	9201	5.9	330
Central-west	24.8	14115	1.0	350
Murrumbidgee	22.0	12728	1.0	280
South-east	21.1	12344	0.9	260
Murray	19.6	8685	1.0	170
Northern	18.6	16138	2.9	300
Illawarra	17.6	26657[b]	0.5	470
Hunter	15.7	38259	0.4	600
Mid-north coast	15.4	14320	1.6	220
Richmond-Tweed	11.4	11419	1.2	130

Notes: [a] Excludes migratory and Lord Howe Island populations of girls aged 10–19 years.
[b] Includes 1638 girls from Wollondilly due to coding difficulty.
[c] Girls born in years 1960–64.

Table 3.2 Detection rates for female delinquency in the LGAs with the largest Aboriginal populations in NSW[a]

LGA	Detection rate	Female population aged 10–19 years	Per cent of population[b] Aboriginal	No. of delinquent girls
Bourke	153.5	391	19.0	60
Walgett	113.9	527	16.1	60
Brewarrina	80.0	251	30.1	20
Central Darling	76.6	261	18.1	20
Moree	50.0	1592	11.5	80

Notes: [a] Largest in a proportional sense—not raw figures.
[b] Population data based on 1981 census. The census significantly underestimates the number of Aboriginal residents in these LGAs. More realistic calculations estimate that about half of the residents in these five LGAs are Aboriginal (Cunneen and Robb, 1987).

times greater in Walgett than for non-Aboriginal youth. (Cunneen, Robb, 1987, p. 143)

In addition to these high charge rates, Aboriginal youth constitute about 25 per cent of inmates in NSW juvenile correctional institutions yet comprise less than two per cent of the total population of the State (Youth Justice Project, 1990).

Studies comparing prosecution and incarceration rates of Aboriginal youth to non-Aboriginal youth in other Australian States have also reported massive variations between the two groups. In Western Australia, Aboriginal youth are over-represented in detention by a factor of sixty-two, in New South Wales by a factor of sixteen and in Queensland by a factor of twelve (Cunneen, 1991, p. 16). Aboriginal youth comprise only 1.2 per cent of the Western Australian population, but account for 19.6 per cent of appearances in the State courts (Freiberg *et al.* 1988, p. 49). In Queensland, Aboriginal youth are seven times more likely to be placed in custody than non-Aboriginal youth (D'Souza, 1990, p. 4). In the Northern Territory, Aboriginal youth have accounted for almost 45 per cent of all cases appearing before the courts since 1983 (D'Souza, 1990, p. 4). In South Australia, Aboriginal youth comprise only 1.2 per cent of those aged between ten and seventeen years yet they account for 4.1 per cent of appearances before Juvenile Aid Panels, 14 per cent of court appearances and 31.9 per cent of all youth sentenced to detention centres (Gayle and Wundersitz, 1985, pp. 213–14). The most significant finding of this latter study is that Aboriginal youth come to be increasingly over-represented as they move up through the hierarchy of punishments available to the Children's Courts. The authors of this South Australian study suggest that the reasons lie in the way in which the justice system operates and particularly in the way in which the police use their discretionary powers of apprehension and arrest. They concluded that:

> Despite the far-reaching legislative changes to the juvenile justice system in South Australia, and despite huge financial expenditures in Aboriginal welfare and legal services during the past one and a half decades, we still seem to be a long way from securing any real reduction in the degree of Aboriginal over-representation in the justice system. (Gayle and Wundersitz, 1987, p. 133)

A Royal Commission into Aboriginal Deaths in Custody (RCIADIC) was established in October 1987 to investigate the circumstances of Aboriginal deaths in custody. One major finding of the Royal Commission was not that Aborigines died in custody at a rate greater than non-Aborigines but that they were twenty-nine times more likely, on a national average, to be detained in custody. The pattern of deaths between the groups differs, however, with the majority of non-Aboriginal deaths occurring in prison while Aboriginal deaths occurred in police custody (Muirhead, 1989). One fifth of those detained in custody were under the age of nineteen years (McDonald, 1990, p. 11). Another important finding of the RCIADIC is that Aboriginal women were even more over-represented than Aboriginal men in custody. Aboriginal women comprise nearly 50 per cent of all female custodies and almost 14 per cent of all female prisoners in Australia although they account for less than 1.5 per cent of the national female population (McDonald, 1990, p. 9; Biles 1989, p. 10).

To reduce the number of Aboriginal deaths in custody the RCIADIC recommended that the rate of incarceration for both the adult and juvenile Aboriginal population be reduced dramatically (Recommendation 1 of *Interim Report* and Recommendation 92 of *National Report*). The Royal Commission suggested a range of initiatives to reduce the number of Aboriginal youth who come into custody including: the use of summons rather than arrest; greater use of bail rather than detention on remand; greater use of diversionary schemes such as police cautioning and juvenile aid panels; greater involvement of the Aboriginal community in the criminalisation process; enhanced career structures for police officers committed to deterrence; changes in police culture enabling police to resist the demands of white communities to 'go hard' on Aboriginal youth; separating justice from welfare to break the nexus between poverty, race and criminality; internal changes to departmental policy and resources to allow greater flexibility and encourage the maximum contact between Aboriginal youth in custody and their families; and greater employment opportunities and leisure activities available to Aboriginal youth in their communities (Wootten, 1991, pp. 347–57).

During the five-year period between 1982 and 1987 there was a 68 per cent increase in Aboriginal imprisonment rates in Australia (Biles, 1989, p. 5). Significantly, the Royal Commission findings have not yet had a positive impact as Aboriginal imprisonment rates have since increased by a further 25 per cent nationally. In New South Wales the proportion of Aboriginal prisoners rose by 80 per cent, in Victoria by 75 per cent, in Western Australia by 24 per cent, in South Australia by 2 per cent and in Tasmania by 43 per cent (Cunneen, 1992, p.351). There were marginal decreases in both Queensland and the Northern Territory of 2 per cent (Cunneen, 1992, p. 351).

During this period of escalating Aboriginal imprisonment rates in NSW, both the State Liberal Coalition and Labor parties tried to outdo each other in terms of promises for tougher sentencing for offenders (Hogg, 1988). One of the outcomes was the introduction of the *Sentencing Act* 1989 (NSW). A major consequence of this Act has been a massive increase in the adult prison population. For youth in detention, the median duration of a term of committal increased from 98 days to 182 (Wootten, 1991, p. 354). Given the massive disproportion of Aboriginal youth in custody, the *Sentencing Act* 1989 has escalated their rate of incarceration in NSW.

Hal Wootten, one of the Commissioners inquiring into Aboriginal Deaths in Custody, has described the number of Aboriginal juveniles in custody as a national crisis by any standard (Wootten, 1991, p. 346). The Commissioner noted that the over-representation of Aboriginal youth in maximum security units was even higher than in other institutions: 'The proportion of Aboriginals in Endeavour House [a maximum security unit] at times before it was closed reached 60 per cent, a figure attributed to their propensity to abscond' (Wootten, 1991, p. 346). The Commissioner then goes on to say:

> While only one of the deaths which I investigated, that of Thomas Carr, was a juvenile, 8 were of persons who had been first charged when they were under 14, and 9 others were first charged when they were less than 19 years old. At least 8 had spent time in juvenile justice institutions. Generally the cases demonstrate the failure of the juvenile justice system to achieve any success in dealing with children and youths who come to the attention of the juvenile welfare or justice systems. (Wootten, 1991, p. 346)

The visibility of otherness and the invisibility of criminalisation

One explanation for the massive level of over-representation of Aboriginal people in the criminal justice system is that it is largely the result of over-policing. Evidence of over-policing is calculated in a number of ways, but usually in terms of police strength and the proportion of public order offences attributed to Aboriginal offenders. Wilcannia, for example, has a population of 1000, 800 of whom are Aboriginal and a police to population ratio six times the State average (Wootten, 1991, p. 301). Street offences, such as offensive behaviour and unseemly words, constitute the largest category of offences laid against Aboriginal people arrested in the town (Wilson, 1988, p. 3). Rates of offending for trivial public order offences (mostly for swearing at police or refusing to obey police instructions) cannot be disconnected from the policing strategies which produce them as most of these offences arise in the context of pro-active policing—of attempts by police to clear the streets of Aboriginal residents (Wootten, 1991, p. 301).

Clear-up rates may well be higher among Aboriginal communities because of the greater police strength in these communities. However, higher rates of conviction among Aboriginal people for offences such as theft, assault and murder are not easily explained as being simply the products of over-policing. The concept of over-policing eschews the reality of violence, and domestic violence in particular that occurs in Aboriginal communities. The problem for Aboriginal women may, in fact, be under-policing, that is a reluctance on the part of the police to intervene in domestic violence situations even when requested to do so (Payne, 1992, pp. 33). Another way of taking up the issue is to examine the localised policing strategies deployed in specific towns like Bourke and Wilcannia where threshold decisions are routinely made to regulate the visibility of Aboriginal populations in those towns.[1]

Public order offences

Five of the six Aboriginal girls from my case history sample had been convicted of public order offences. In all five cases a list of allegations about their unruly public conduct was presented to the court as evidence of female delinquency of one kind or another. The list of allegations included the following forms of conduct: 'hanging around the streets' 'with youths adversely known to the department or the police', 'without adult supervision', 'making a public nuisance of themselves' and 'showing no respect for authority'. There are several important points that need to be made about policing strategies which use public order offences as a way of removing Aboriginal youth from the streets.

The first is that the marginality of Aboriginal youth makes them more visible to the policing authorities and hence much more accessible to prosecution for public order offences. While the private sanctuary of the domestic sphere affords young people a measure of invisibility and hence insulation against detection for minor delinquencies, the visibility of otherness has the opposite effect. It predisposes the youth of marginal populations to much higher levels of detection for essentially the same conduct. It then follows that the marginality of Aboriginal youth to mainstream social, employment and educational institutions, disproportionately predisposes them to the disciplinary gaze of the justice authorities. The fact that the bulk of matters for which Aboriginal youth and adults appear before the courts involve petty public order offences, such as drunkenness, unseemly words and offensive behaviour, resisting arrest and refusing to leave premises adds a good deal of empirical substance to this argument. That Aboriginal communities have historically been policed as public and not private spheres compounds the extent of their visibility to the authorities, and hence their level of criminalisation. It is for these reasons that the Aboriginal youth and their families who live in communities policed in this way come to be regarded as being 'police property' (Hogg, 1991, p. 16).

Lucy's case provides a clear example of the consequences that the visibility of marginality has for young people living in Aboriginal communities. Lucy[2] was apprehended with five others aged between eleven and fourteen years for drinking alcohol around a camp fire one Friday night. They were detected as the result of a routine police check of 'the reserve', explained in the following extract from the arresting police officer's statement to the Children's Court.

> On the arrival of the police the majority of the children decamped to the nearby bush . . . However some children remained . . . and the child before the court Lucy was affected by intoxicating liquor . . . Police inquiries later revealed, sir, the children had accumulated together what little money they had and this was an amount of $5.00 approximately. Then two of the children went to a hotel in the area seeking the aid of an adult person they knew in the hotel, obtained a flagon of wine and seven cans of beer.
>
> They returned to (the back of the reserve) where the children began drinking. Eddie (one of the children) ended up in hospital with alcohol poisoning. (Sworn Statement, 6 July 1976)

In cross-examination, the constable was asked, 'You agree as far that this was an isolated incident and not a regular occurrence?' to which the constable replied, 'It would appear so, sir, yes' (Court Transcripts, 6 July 1976). Despite this mitigating evidence all six of the apprehended Aboriginal children were committed to institutions. The youngest was eleven the eldest was sixteen, one of whom was Lucy.

A second and related point is that the proportion of public order offences attributed to Aboriginal youth is also partly a consequence of the invisibility of summary justice. Because the criminal justice system at this 'less visible though more busy end is predominantly directed at the management of social marginality' (Hogg, 1991, p. 5), its effects are felt disproportionately by some groups, as evidenced by the massive over-representation of youth from Aboriginal communities and housing commission areas in summary offence categories. The relative invisibility of summary justice provides a buffer against public scrutiny and accountability. The invisibility of criminalisation at this level therefore constitutes, as Hogg suggests:

> . . . a domain of social control that is restricted in its intensity but which exchanges a power of severity for an extensive and regularised reach into the social body, freed from many of the trappings and protections of law. What is lost in severity is gained in autonomy. In vital respects it has taken the issue of deaths in custody to open up this realm of penality to some scrutiny, to demonstrate that the workings and effects of criminal justice in its summary mode, are anything but trivial. (Hogg, 1991, p. 5)

Sally Cole's experience with the justice system illustrates the point made by Hogg in the passage above. Over a period of less than a year Sally appeared before the Children's Court four times for drunkenness and once for unseemly words. In isolation none of these trivial offences could justify Sally's committal to an institution. Yet their cumulation over the period of one year allowed the magistrate to justify sentencing her to an institution on the fourth occasion. Summary justice, as a form regularised to reach into Sally's life, had anything but a trivial impact on it.

One final point to be considered in relation to the policing strategies which use public order offences to criminalise Aboriginal girls looks at the way in which their use of public space upsets the normative boundaries of that space. This disruption then inevitably brings some girls into conflict with the authorities, with charges being laid and so on. In several instances the persistence of 'hanging out' in streets, parks and shopping centres led to court action against several of the Aboriginal girls in my study who were each charged with various public order or welfare offences. It seems that their only 'crime' was that their social visibility contested the normative use of that space as places for consumption, family outings and picnics. However, the mere public display of the black female body was sufficient enough in itself to be regarded as 'harmful to the local community'—an often quoted phrase in Court Reports. One of the Aboriginal girls whose case I examined was actually taken into custody because of fears that respectable parents and citizens of the town would be upset at the prospect of white boys being seduced by an Aboriginal girl who hangs around the street. Upon her committal to an institution, details of her offence were described in the following terms:

> The young person would leave places of residence and engage in sexual intercourse with a number of boys. She was not of good behaviour. (Record of Case on Committal to Institution, 3 May 1980)

Upon being taken into custody this girl was found to have syphilis. A training program then commenced during which she was:

> . . . taught the basic rudiments of contraception and is presently on the pill. She has been advised to see the local sister when necessary, and attempts have been made to develop more personal responsibility and restraint in her relationships with boys. All will be to little avail after her inevitable 'Discharge Celebration' down at the local. (Resident Psychologist Review of Inmate, 6 August 1980)

In these discourses Aboriginal girls are made morally responsible for the sexual conduct of white boys and the fears of white parents. It is they who are the source of moral decay and venereal disease, not their male partners. It is they who must bear the sole responsibility for sexual hygiene and contraception not their companions. If sex with white boys does occur it is they who must be equipped with the contraceptive knowledge not to fall pregnant. It is Aboriginal girls who are made the guardians of white racial purity through the disciplining of their bodies, preferably by keeping them out of the sight of designing young white boys overcome by supposedly natural 'hydraulic' urges. This is why the social visibility of Aboriginal girls contests the normative boundaries of public space and why such visibility then attracts an inordinate degree of police attention.

In a much less obvious way, the policing of public space occurs through such mechanisms as bail or probation conditions, which specify that being of 'good behaviour' means avoiding 'other youths of adverse reputation' who are 'known to the authorities'. Given the massive proportion of Aboriginal juveniles with criminal records in localities such as Wilcannia, most Aboriginal teenagers in such towns would have associations with 'youth adversely known to the department or the police'. In Wilcannia during 1987, for example,

45 per cent of the town's male Aboriginal juvenile population were arrested (Wilson, 1988). Few, if any, Aboriginal youth in these communities are insulated from the taint of the criminal justice system. Mere kin and cultural relationships expose them to the risk of penal identification. The implication is clear. Unless Aboriginal youth extricate themselves from public associations with kin and from participating in local youth cultures, which almost invariably occur in public space, they are highly susceptible to further court action for breaching probation conditions.

Truancy and child welfare proceedings

The criminalisation of otherness operates in many other contexts in which Aboriginal girls are brought before the Children's Courts and not only in those which seek to regulate their public conduct. In what follows I consider the criminalising effects that truancy and other child welfare provisions have had on Aboriginal girls and their families.

While the relationship between schooling and juvenile justice is considered more fully in the following chapter it is appropriate to consider here its specific criminalising effect on Aboriginal girls. In addition to the public order offences referred to above, five of the six Aboriginal girls whose case histories I examined had appeared before the Children's Court at one time or another for irregular school attendance. Jenny, a pseudonym for one of these girls, was committed to State wardship for being uncontrollable. A 'poor school attendance record', 'stealing 50 cents from a teacher's desk which she spent on food', and 'behavioural problems at school' were among a set of uncontrollable behaviours attributed to her during this court appearance. Initial court action against Debbie, another Aboriginal girl whose case was examined, also arose out of poor school attendance. This girl was eventually committed to wardship and forcibly severed from her kin and community for a breach of probation which involved, among other things as serious as smoking and bed wetting, truanting from school. Lucy, whose case was discussed earlier, spent a second period in detention because of court action taken against her for school default. Most of her siblings had been under supervision for school default and her younger brother and older sister had also been committed to institutions for this reason. For Terese, truancy and 'educational retardation' were important deciding factors in her committal to wardship and subsequent committal to an institution. For Sally, although her Juvenile Criminal Index states that she was committed to an institution for the offence of drunkenness, her previous expulsion from school for disruptive behaviour and non-attendance was a factor used to justify a period of 'environmental manipulation' in an appropriate training school. The only Aboriginal girl in the study not to appear before the court at some time or another for charges related to truancy was, in fact, never sent to school due to a physical birth disability.

Prior to the 1940s, the attendance of Aboriginal children in State schools was actually prohibited by State and Commonwealth policies of racial segregation (Fletcher, 1975, p. 30). New South Wales was one of the first Australian States to reverse racial segregation in favour of absorption through the implementation of programs in Aboriginal education (McConnochie, 1982, p. 23). There was general agreement among educationalists of the time that assimilation was most likely to succeed if racial integration began at an early age. Hence schools have a history of being used as instruments in the political objective of assimilation (Fletcher, 1975, p. 30), which some see as form of cultural genocide.

Given the historical context in which Aboriginal children have been, or rather have not been, schooled it is reasonable to argue, as Cowlishaw does, that truancy expresses a legitimate dislike of school (Cowlishaw, 1988, p. 235). High schools with large proportions of Aboriginal students have the highest truancy rates and lowest retention rates of schools in the State of New South Wales. Bourke High School, for example, has a truancy rate of 22.5 days per term per child (Cunneen and Robb, 1987, p. 32). Court action for truancy has culturally specific consequences for Aboriginal youth. It effectively blames, punishes and locates the source of difficulty with Aboriginal children and their families eschewing any social responsibility for the forms of racism institutionalised in schooling. Their experience of racism is exacerbated while the issue of racism is simply erased. This can be more clearly understood by examining a case where this has occurred.

The circumstances in which Lucy was committed to an institution for being intoxicated around a camp fire have already been discussed. She was later recommitted to an institution for truancy. The superintendent of the corrective institution to which Lucy was sent wrote the following comments in a School Placement Report upon her release.

> Lucy is an attractive aboriginal [sic] girl of average intelligence and above average athletic ability. In the past many factors have led to her truanting from school, not the least of which was her disinterest. If placement is to be successful Lucy will need a lot of support and encouragement as she is inclined to be lazy and introspective.
> (School Placement Report, 16/1/78)

In this document, and there were many others like them in Lucy's institutional file, Lucy is made to appear responsible for her educational under-achievement, her disinterest in school and her truancy. In other documents Lucy's mother is blamed for not sending her children to school. For reasons already argued the truancy of Aboriginal children, with or without the tacit approval of parents, is an understandable response to the forms of racism experienced at school. There is plenty of evidence to suggest that racism in State schools has anything but abated. A recent Education Department inquiry into racism at Casino High School largely substantiated allegations made against teachers by Aboriginal students. That inquiry has recommended that *all* teachers at the school seek voluntary transfers (*Sydney Morning Herald*, 5 November 1992).

I will now consider how court action through child welfare proceedings can as well have the effect of criminalising otherness, in this case Aboriginality. Prior to 1969, such criminalisation was carried out as part of a eugenicist policy of assimilation. Since then, Aboriginal children have been removed from their families on the basis of science, not race: a science which calculates family pathology in terms of deviation from statistical norms (Rose, 1984, p. 123). The following explains how this shift in child welfare intervention techniques has occurred.

Prior to the abolition of the Aborigines Welfare Board in 1969, Aboriginal children could be removed from their families simply on the basis of race.[3] The control and legislative power to remove Aboriginal children was the sole responsibility of specialised departments such as the Aborigines Welfare Board and of specialised institutions such as Aboriginal reserves, Aboriginal boys' homes and Aboriginal girls' homes (Morris, 1989). Aboriginal reserves are the historical residue of colonial practices toward Aboriginal people in New South Wales. They were primarily sites for the institutionalisation of Aboriginal people so that they could be managed, 'civilised' and assimilated (Morris, 1989). In recent years, those reserves that have not been sold off have been handed over to the Aboriginal residents. A key aspect of this so-called civilising process involved the extensive removal of Aboriginal children from their homes, particularly, but not necessarily, those children of mixed racial parentage (Goodall, 1990, p. 6). The impact of such policies on Aboriginal communities is, of course, 'incalculable'. The history of the stolen generations is now well documented (Read, undated; Edwards and Read, 1989; Goodall, 1988, p. 5). Read estimates that almost 6000 children were removed from their Aboriginal families over the period from 1883 to 1969 (Read, undated, p. 9). Goodall estimates that up until 1929 as many as one in three Aboriginal children were taken away by the child welfare system (Goodall, 1988, p. 5). Most of these children were girls who could be apprenticed as domestic servants (Goodall, 1990). It was common practice to foster such children to non-Aboriginal families or place them in special institutions set up for Aboriginal girls, such as Cootamundra Girls Home.

Only one of the Aboriginal girls in my study was made a ward of the Aborigines Welfare Board (under Section 13A of the 1909 *Aborigines Protection Act*). At the age of one, her mother had taken her to the local doctor for treatment and, without any knowledge or warning, she was literally stolen out of the back door of the surgery and taken to the local 'welfare office'. This girl remained in the care of the department until the age of twenty-one, during which time she had no contact with her Aboriginal family or community. She spent her early childhood years in the care of non-Aboriginal foster families and was committed to a psychiatric institution in her early adolescence. At the age of 21, when released from the care of the department, this girl was a long-term psychiatric inmate.

In 1969, with the dissolution of the Aborigines Welfare Board, the power to remove Aboriginal children from their families shifted to the New South Wales Social and Child Welfare Department (under the *Child Welfare Act*, 1939 (NSW)). While race has been erased from the statutes as a legitimate ground for taking Aboriginal children into custody, because family pathology is diagnosed in terms of deviation from the norm Aboriginal children have continued to be removed from their families by the welfare authorities. Aboriginal families have been drawn into the practices of therapeutic familialism and their children have been drawn into the discourses of childhood health, education and psychology (in the same way as white children). Those who fail to adequately provide for the needs of children, that is those with less than adequate material living standards or those who fail to send their children to school, can be defined as dysfunctional. These evaluations, prescribed by the scientific discourses of childhood, make Aboriginal children the legitimate targets of welfare intervention which seeks their removal on the basis of competence and not race.

Of the six Aboriginal girls whose cases I examined, all were variously described in court documents as coming from either 'dysfunctional families' or 'bad home environments'. Three were forcibly severed from their kin through wardship proceedings under Section 72(o) of the *Child Welfare Act* 1939 (NSW) as neglected children, in the same way that white children were committed to State care. Instead of being sent to establishments catering specifically for Aboriginal children, they were now sent to a range of ward hostels, foster families and even sheltered workshops for the mentally deficient, to which non-Aboriginal children coming into State care were also sent. Thus the contemporary context has witnessed a diffusion of the sites of bureaucratic control of Aboriginal families and an intensification of the mutual interplay between judicial and extra-judicial agencies in that process.

Mary's history is a case in point. Mary had lived in what court documents described as a 'dirt floor shack on the reserve' with 'a dozen other siblings'. She was taken into wardship on the basis that she was neglected by her parents. The court was told that there were more than two children per room and that the State could provide Mary with a better standard of care than her family. In these therapeutic discourses, living arrangements, family cultures and parenting practices, particularly those circumscribed by marginality and poverty, represent the 'other'—those 'bad families' who, from the vantage point of such discourses, are incapable of raising children without supervision or 'assistance'. That the family was impoverished and the home overcrowded was enough to satisfy the Children's Court that Mary was being neglected. Her family could not, according to the department, adequately provide for her needs. The family was assessed as dysfunctional and the parents as incompetent. The requirements now existed for the Children's Court to dispense with parental rights and order the family's children to be taken into State care.

Once in the welfare system Aboriginal girls almost invariably enter the fast track from care to detention. All four Aboriginal girls in my study who were made State wards (one under the 1909 Act, the other three under the 1939 Act) were placed in an array of non-Aboriginal foster families and ward establishments. Three were subsequently sentenced to juvenile institutions for offences involving their absconding from ward establishments with the purpose of returning to their families and Aboriginal communities. Aboriginal children made wards are then particularly vulnerable, as wards are more generally, to being dragged into the orbit of criminal justice agencies through the nexus that exists between welfare and justice. The mechanics of this nexus are considered more fully in the final chapter. For the purposes of the argument developed here this vulnerability may be more clearly understood if we examine a specific instance.

In a little over a year after being made a state ward, Terese appeared before the Children's Court a further four times—three were for stealing money with the purpose of returning to her family and Aboriginal community in the north-west of rural NSW. During that year she had been placed in six different ward establishments and two sheltered workshops, from which she absconded at least a dozen times. Each time she endeavoured to return to her family. On one occasion she was committed to an institution for stealing money which she used to purchase a train ticket back home. She appealed against her committal but lost. The supervising district officer presented a lengthy report to the District Court outlining the details of her family background, previous court appearances, schooling, employment history and placements by the department. The report described in detail the many failed attempts to place Terese in a variety of departmental establishments, six in all. Terese had absconded from all at least once, and from some, several times. The District Court was then informed that:

> During the above placements, Terese has had a history of absconding if she was not happy with the surroundings. To my knowledge she has not been a behaviour problem whilst under departmental care. Terese is a very quiet lass who finds difficulty in settling into new situations, particularly if she feels there is any possibility of her returning to the care of her relatives. She has difficulty in accepting the decisions of this department, re her placement, and usually resorts to absconding from any situation not to her liking . . . Terese is a very quietly spoken aboriginal [sic] girl who identifies strongly with the Aboriginal community and particularly with her own family. In her own way Terese is quietly determined to have her own way and will often use manipulative behaviour, such as absconding to achieve her own desires . . .
> Having worked with Terese for the main part of this year I do not feel that any of the alternatives suggested by the lass are feasible nor has it been possible to find an alternative placement in which Terese would receive (and accept) necessary supervision and guidance. (District Court Report, 23 June 1978)

The removal of Terese from her family through welfare proceedings created an ongoing relationship of tension between her and the welfare authorities, which set in motion the train of events described in this document. The escalation of this tension, and particularly Terese's determination to return to her family, finally led to her committal to a detention centre. Her case is a clear example of the mutual dependence between judicial and extra-judicial agencies whereby professionals in social work and psychology are called upon to assess family background, to diagnose problems and to offer the court a 'remedy'. Her case is also a particularly transparent example of the way resistance to forms of therapeutic intervention can be defined as individual pathology sufficient to justify incarceration. Terese refused to comply with departmental instructions about how, where and with whom she ought to live. This resistance was then defined in departmental terms as the offence of 'absconding', for which she was eventually committed to an institution.

The evidence of the Royal Commission into Aboriginal Deaths

in Custody suggests that Terese's negative experience of the welfare system is not an isolated or exceptional one. In his report on the death of Malcolm Smith, Commissioner Wootten claims that Malcolm's death is the story of a life destroyed 'in large measure by the regular operation of the system of self-righteous, heartless and racist destruction of Aboriginal families that went on under the name of protection or welfare well into the second half of this century' (Wootten, 1989, p. 1). Malcolm Smith was made a state ward at the age of eleven. He did not see his family for another eight years and spent most of that time in juvenile corrective institutions. In the remaining years of his adult life he spent only a few months outside prison before eventually committing suicide while in custody in 1983.

Criminalising otherness

The over-policing of Aboriginal communities contributes in no small measure to the over-representation of Aboriginal youth in the juvenile justice system. However, it has to be recognised that this level of over-policing is as much the result of the stress that policing strategies place on controlling public conduct as it is the result of conscious decisions to subject Aboriginal communities to disproportionate degrees of policing. Similarly, the over-zealous removal of Aboriginal children from their communities is as much the result of providing 'welfare assistance' to 'failing families' as it is the consequence of deliberate and overtly racist child welfare policies. To construe the over-representation of Aboriginal girls, or boys for that matter, in the juvenile justice system simply as a matter of over-policing or over-zealousness on the part of welfare workers runs the risks of being seduced into a 'rotten apple' theory of racism and also being led astray by naive attempts to remove those rotten apples (Henriques, 1984, p. 60). The issue is more complex, more subtle and more deeply embedded than this.

Techniques of welfare intervention have shifted significantly this century such that race is no longer sufficient grounds to remove Aboriginal children from their families. Essentialist readings of the operation of the welfare and justice agencies have consequently lost their power to explain how Aboriginal children nevertheless continue to be targeted under a new form of welfare intervention which makes them objects of assistance on the basis of family dysfunction, not race. Because pathology is diagnosed in these new discourses as deviations from the cultural specificity of the statistical norm (the norm being non-Aboriginal cultural and familial relations), the criminalisation of otherness, in this case

Aboriginality, is an obvious consequence. In other words, Aboriginal families have been drawn into a network of strategies for governing family life in the same way as non-Aboriginal families. The way in which these new strategies of governance (that is deficit discourses) work in the administration of juvenile justice is an issue of considerable importance which is dealt with in the final chapter. The next three chapters examine how the mechanisms of juvenile justice translate otherness, at school, in families and at play, into evidence of delinquency and family dysfunction.

4 Schools, sex and juvenile justice

> As a rule, truancy is little thought of, but in actual fact, it is usually the first step on the downward stair to crime.
> (Cyril Burt, *The Delinquent*, 1925, p. 445)

The two preceding chapters considered, but finally rejected the proposition that there is an essentialised relation between the administration of juvenile justice and either gender or race such that the workings of juvenile justice can be explained as a form of either sexism or racism or as a mixture of both. The detection rates for female delinquency suggest that juvenile criminalisation is a much more specific, rather than generalised process. Not every girl who flouts the norms of adolescent femininity and chastity ends up in an institution or before the courts. Yet this is the logical conclusion of the sexualisation thesis. The recruitment of girls into the justice system is inexplicable in terms of an argument which posits the root cause in some over-arching form of female oppression and then caricatures the role of juvenile justice in this sexualisation process as being the loyal servant of patriarchal masters. Behind the veneer of this seamless web of repression everything distinct disappears, including the differential impact of juvenile justice on the lives of young women. Girls are differentiated in terms of their vulnerability to the control and scope of the justice authorities.

In this and the following two chapters I attempt to provide an explanation for some of these discrepancies by focusing on *how* specific girls, mostly from Aboriginal and socially disadvantaged backgrounds, come into the orbit of criminalising agencies and by looking at what happens to them and their families when they do. The school, the family and leisure activities are the three principal sites and means through which the girls in this study were channelled into the formal mechanisms of juvenile justice. This chapter deals with the position of schools in the manufacture of female delinquency. Chapters 5 and 6 deal with the place of families and leisure in that process.

Compulsory schooling regulations

The school has only become a site for channelling youth into the juvenile justice system with the passing of legislation making school attendance compulsory. Attendance at school has not always been compulsory and indeed the legislative basis for taking court action against truants and their parents has undergone repeated change during the last decade. However, for most of this century education has been compulsory for children under the age of fifteen years in most Australian States, as elsewhere in the industrialised world.

Education was first made compulsory in NSW (except for Aboriginal children) with the passing of the *Education Act* 1880 (NSW) (Chisholm, 1987, p. 84). The enforcement of regular school attendance has since operated under several other pieces of legislation. One of these was the *Public Instruction Act* 1915 (NSW) under which parents could be fined for not sending their children to school. A perusal of the Annual Reports of the department confirm that very few parents have been fined for school default. Rather, the bulk of court action involving school default over the last thirty years has been directed at children, not parents, and proceeded with under Section 72(o) of the *Child Welfare Act* 1939 (NSW). Under this section of the Act a child who, without lawful excuse, fails to attend school regularly could be dealt with as a neglected or uncontrollable child and thus sentenced to an institution or put on probation as a juvenile offender. Until recently the department detained truants in special institutions known as Training Schools for Truants (for example, Ormond and Anglewood as they were formerly operated). Placement in this system was discretionary and it was not unusual for truants to be sent to detention centres for juvenile offenders. Truants released under probation were usually required to abide by a set of conditions similar to those for juvenile offenders—regular school attendance, acceptance of departmental supervision and good behaviour. As a condition of release under probation, truants were sometimes also required to attend Child Guidance Clinics, psychiatric counselling or special after school programs. Section 72(o) of the *Child Welfare Act* 1939 permitted extra-judicial agencies, such as psychologists and district officers, a great deal of discretion in dealing with truants in much the same way as juvenile offenders.

On 18 January 1988 a package of new Acts replaced the *Child*

Welfare Act 1939 (NSW).[1] Under the new legislation truancy ceased to constitute sufficient legal grounds for juvenile justice intervention. It had become obvious that the Department of Youth and Community Services (YACS) which administered juvenile justice over the previous decade had given truancy a low priority from the early 1980s. In fact, YACS had ceased policing truancy in 1985, several years before the new Acts removed it as an offence. This dynamic is clearly discernible in Figure 4.1 which depicts court appearances for truancy in NSW from 1965 to 1988. During this time a Home School Liaison program was instituted as a Labor government initiative directing the responsibility for truancy squarely upon the shoulders of the Education Department (Blackmore, 1989, p. 112).

A conservative coalition government was elected in the State in 1988. That government then embarked on a law and order campaign toughening jail sentences and introducing draconian legislation such as the *Summary Offences Act* 1988 (NSW) and *The Sentencing Act* 1989 (NSW) (Hogg and Brown, 1991). As part of a wider law and order policy which involved tougher responses to juvenile offenders, the conservative government debated and passed the *Education Reform Act* 1990 (NSW) which reinstated truancy as an offence, under Part 5 of that Act. The legislation allows for court action to

Figure 4.1   Truancy by sex, NSW Children's Courts 1960–88

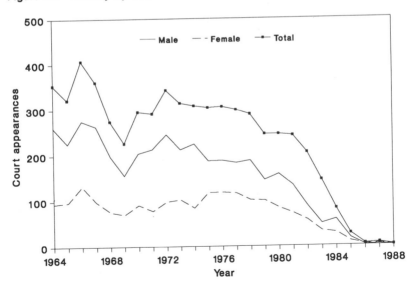

Source: YACS Annual Reports.

be taken against a child who without lawful excuse fails to attend school. The Act also makes provision for fines of up to $2000 for parents who fail to send their children to school. There was considerable turmoil over the reintroduction of truancy as an offence culminating in the stalling of the bill's early passage through the upper house (*Sydney Morning Herald*, 17 November 1988; *Sydney Morning Herald*, 4 May 1989). In laying down the politically expedient groundwork for the reintroduction of truancy as an offence the then newly elected police minister in the conservative government was quoted in the press as saying that:

> . . . truancy has emerged as a leading social problem. There is little doubt that young people playing truant are contributing in quite large measure to certain categories of crime, including such offences as car theft and breaking and entering. (*Sydney Morning Herald*, 17 November 1988)

The renewed emphasis placed on enforcing compulsory schooling regulations through the juvenile justice apparatus represents a major reversal of the policy initiatives adopted by the outgoing Labor government in relation to truants. It is significant that an emphasis on truancy and discipline problems in schools has occurred within a political context of massive spending cuts in public education, resulting in increased class sizes and fewer teachers to deal with discipline problems in schools. Indeed, one of the purposes of this chapter is to convey a number of serious objections to managing truancy through mechanisms which resort to coercive juvenile justice intervention.

It would be naive to assume that all truants are detected, or that when caught that they are treated in an identical way. Nor should it be assumed that *all* or indeed many schools have recommenced using legislative provisions for dealing with truancy. Given the apparent success of the Home School Liaison program most will hopefully resist resorting to judicial solutions for managing truants. The problem is that such an option still exists for the few schools which choose to be so punitive and, on past experience, these schools tend to be located in the far west of the State where up to half of the student body are Aboriginal. So, although the cases in this study occurred a decade or more ago, given the current emphasis on enforcing school attendance through mechanisms of juvenile justice the issues they raise are just as important today.

Girls, truancy and juvenile justice: some case studies

Court action, either for truancy or involving truancy, was taken against forty-three of the fifty-nine girls in this case study sample.

Given the sheer volume of data it is impractical to present all the relevant material from all forty-three cases here. Instead, the argument developed summarises this material in the context of analysing details from several specific cases.

In twenty-four of the forty-three cases where truancy was a major component in a repertoire of delinquent behaviours presented to the court, the first encounter with the justice authorities was actually *initiated* by the school. In the remaining sixteen cases contact with the justice authorities was initiated in a variety of other ways: some came into contact with the authorities through the probation of other siblings, others through informants such as neighbours, relatives or professionals of various kinds (doctors, nurses or social workers). In only three of forty-three cases did the justice authorities confine their concern to schooling. These cases were atypical because the behaviour of these three girls outside school was not considered delinquent. For these girls their persistent absences from school constituted the sole basis for court action.

It must be emphasised that Sandra's case, which I use for the purpose of raising a general issue about the way in which the enforcement of compulsory schooling regulations affects socially disadvantaged families, was less typical of the others in that the justice authorities were basically *only* concerned with her school default. This over-emphasis is partly addressed by using the case notes of other girls in the latter part of the discussion. These cases were more typical in that the justice authorities were concerned with conduct both in and out of school and not just with the fact that these girls had failed to attend school.

Sandra had lived most of her childhood in an extended family arrangement with her mother, six siblings and a few nephews and nieces. Her father had died several years earlier. The family was supported by the widow's pension and resided in what court documents described as 'an old timber three bedroom dwelling with outside toilet' (Record of Case on Committal to an Institution, 5 June 1975). At the age of thirteen years Sandra was committed to an institution under Section 72(o) of the *Child Welfare Act* 1939 (NSW) for failing to attend school regularly. Two of her siblings, both brothers, appeared in court with Sandra and were also committed to institutions for truancy. Sandra had twice previously appeared before the Children's Court for irregular school attendance and on both occasions was released on probation. On this occasion the court was told that Sandra had been absent from school for fifty days in the previous year and forty-one days of the first term. The court was also informed that Sandra was content to stay away from school to help her mother who had apparently encouraged her to do so (Court Report, 5 June 1975). It seems that the district officer

supervising this family of persistent school defaulters had become
immensely frustrated by the lack of value attached to education
within this family. This particular anxiety about Sandra's family was
conveyed to the Children's Court in the following way:

> Her (Sandra's) account of why she was charged was confused. She
> couldn't understand the reasons for her committal. She says her
> mother can't either. None of the members of this family can see a
> problem with staying away from school. They refuse to accept that
> it is breaking the law. (Court Report, 5 June 1975)

While in custody Sandra was assessed by a departmental psychologist 'as an under-achiever at school' (Psychological Report, 10
June 1975). The same report also noted that at least four of her
siblings had previously been committed to corrective institutions,
and all seven children in the family had been under supervision for
school default at some time or another (Psychological Report, 10
June 1975).

A major issue to emerge from reading Sandra's notes, and others
like them, is that those already most disadvantaged in the schooling
system are the ones who are propelled into more disciplinary
regimes of control through the enforcement of compulsory schooling
regulations. Sandra, like most of the girls in the study, came from
a socially disadvantaged family background—a single-parent
household and a large number of siblings with little access to
monetary resources or cultural capital from which to build a better
future. A body of educational research suggests that lower
educational outcomes and persistent absences from school are much
more common among working-class children and their families than
among children from more privileged class backgrounds (Connell
et al., 1983; Corrigan, 1979; Willis, 1977). An educational
curriculum geared to university entrance is thought by some
educationalists to make most subjects irrelevant to the concerns of
many students, for whom trade, manual, clerical or domestic
employment is the main destination (Watson, 1985, p. 116). A
disregard for the worth or relevance of education by some children
is one outcome (White, 1990, pp. 95–6); truancy and educational
failure are others (Humphries, 1981, pp. 52–4; Corrigan, 1979, pp.
18–22). Certainly, this was the case for Sandra.

Sandra was not only disadvantaged in the schooling system
because of her social class background but also because of her sex.
It seems she was destined to follow the trajectory of her mother
and older sisters into a future of domesticity for which an education
seemed unnecessary. A body of feminist educational theory suggests
that the schooling system operates to the disadvantage of the female
sex by preparing girls for a future in the home while boys are

prepared for the world of work (MacDonald, 1980, p. 31; Gaskell, 1977, p. 52; Deem, 1980, p. 82). Within this body of feminist theory the non-attendance of girls in formal schooling has been attributed to the demands of domestic and child-care commitments at home (Griffin, 1985, p. 41; McRobbie, 1978, p. 100). The legitimacy of these demands are then said to be endorsed by the technologies of gender inscribed in schools which represent education as less important for girls (Like and Gore, 1992). Pedagogical practices which provide only a narrow range of possible feminine subjectivities are also said to make school boring for many girls. In this pedagogical context it is understandable that girls looking for excitement and adventure are enticed to play truant.

In most of the cases of truancy in this study the school and juvenile justice authorities suspected that girls before the courts for school default had, in fact, stayed home to assist with domestic chores. Jessie's case was represented in precisely these terms in the Court Report quoted below.

> Jessie has been in trouble for poor school attendance since 1976. Her usual pattern is to refuse to attend school in the morning or else she gets up too late to catch the bus. Some of the factors involved in her school refusal appear to be:
> 1. Peer difficulties at school. Jessie's family which is a single parent one, has a bad reputation around the area, with both her mother and brothers coming under the adverse notice of the police. As a result Jessie is the object of quite a deal of teasing and 'stirring' by peers at school. Jessie is easily 'stirred' and this naturally only encourages her peers in their teasing.
> 2. Mrs Samuels, because of work commitments, is not at home to supervise Jessie in getting off to school. As mentioned previously, Jessie often simply stays in bed or gets up too late to catch the bus. There is also some evidence that Jessie's mother and the family tacitly encourage Jessie's non-attendance. For example, the mother often provides the excuses to the school and the district officer for Jessie and her sister frequently gets Jessie to mind her children when Jessie doesn't go to school. (Court Report, 17 August 1980)

The absences of both Sandra and Jessie from school were understood by the authorities as being attributable to domestic demands which had the tacit endorsement from their respective family units. Sandra stayed at home to assist her mother and also her sister with child minding. This girl was caught in a double bind: while her presence at school was not particularly valued, her absences from school could not be tolerated by the school authorities. Sandra's truancy was just as serious as that of her two brothers. Presumably, if the authorities thought Sandra's schooling was unimportant on the basis of her sex, why would they bother taking action against her for non-attendance? I cannot answer this question, however, one plausible explanation is that the school did not want to take the responsibility for trying to provide girls like Sandra with the necessary inducements to attend school. Palming her off onto 'the welfare' provided a way of avoiding any such responsibility.

There was also a suspicion that in many cases those girls not at school were left unsupervised and hence exposed to moral danger.

> This is Jessie's second court appearance. She appeared at the Children's Court previously on a complaint that she was not attending school. The matter was remanded, however during the remand period the girl and her family moved to another State. When the family returned to this area the court action was not proceeded with. Jessie's record of truancy over the past year has been 56 days in term one and 13 days in term two. Although this is Jessie's first court appearance for a considerable time, it is felt that there are a number of reasons which would indicate that a period of committal is necessary. Firstly, Jessie's very poor attendance to date, despite attempts to try and overcome the situation, which means that the girl is working far below her ability. Secondly, her failure to attend school regularly since the first appearance on this matter in May this year and even more recently her failure to attend school any day last week. This would seem to indicate that the girl is not willing to cooperate at all. Finally the fact that Jessie has obviously had sexual intercourse quite recently, and possibly over a period of time. Taking into account the poor family circumstances and the opportunities available while she is truanting there is good reason to believe that if she is allowed to remain at home she will continue to be exposed to moral danger. *Recommend*: Period of committal.
> (Court Report, 9 August 1980)

In cases like these parents were roundly condemned for not delivering their children to school on a regular basis. This raises important issues about the government of children and the respective roles that families and schools have in this process. A recurring point of contention is that, by making attendance at school compulsory, it appears that the school has a declared supremacy over other forms of socialisation such as the family in the government of youth (Donzelot, 1979, p. 201). In some cases, tension between the school authorities and families over matters such as school attendance may result in court action being taken against the children. Terry's case is an example where this occurred. It demonstrates how schools gain normalising access, not just to children, but also to their parents through their child's schooling.

Terry was thirteen-and-a-half years old when the school counsellor requested the local district officer's assistance in dealing with Terry's persistent non-attendance at school. Terry was charged with being uncontrollable and remanded in custody. The court later released her on probation to be of good behaviour, attend school regularly, accept the supervision of the department and attend counselling at a Child Guidance Clinic. In less than two months, however, Terry reappeared before the Children's Court on a complaint that she had breached the terms of probation because she had continued to truant from school and was committed to an institution. The case against her rested on a technical fact that her absences for illness were not endorsed by a medical practitioner. This provided the district officer with grounds to suspect that Terry's mother had again allowed her daughter to stay home without good cause. This evidence was tendered to the Children's Court in the form of a record of interview between Terry and the district officer and stated more bluntly in the accompanying Court Report. The relevant extracts from both documents are quoted below.

DO: 'The school records show that you have not attended school this term. Is that true?'.

Terry: 'I went on the first day of term, but got sent home sick'.

DO: 'Have you got a medical certificate to cover your absences?'.

Terry: 'No'.

DO: 'Have I warned you before about getting medical certificates for having days off school?'.

Terry: 'Yes'. (Record of Interview, 21 September 1979)

Mrs Cowan has been spoken to about the necessity for medical certificates, but to date she had not done so. Mrs Cowan has expressed the feeling that Terry is often not really sick enough to stay home from school, but Mrs Cowan provides the necessary notes. (Court Report, 21 September 1979)

Terry had been absent from school seemingly with her mother's permission. It is in this context that compulsory schooling provisions provide an effective mechanism for gaining access, not just to children, but to families who fail to abide by their civic duty to send their children to school. Compulsory schooling can also provide a mechanism for gaining access to the child's conduct outside school. Terry's case is a good example of this. After coming under the supervision of the department through court action for school default, other dimensions of Terry's life, most notably her leisure activities, soon came under fairly intense scrutiny. This scrutiny led to the supervising district officer laying charges against her for being uncontrollable. The substance of the allegation was represented to the Children's Court in the following manner.

. . . She didn't have permission to my knowledge to be out late the four times in the last three weeks. She was granted a school exemption when she was discharged from Training School. She hasn't worked since. She says recently she has been looking for work but hasn't been able to get any. Most of the time spent at Westpoint is usually spent either wandering around the shops or down at the wine bar which operates there. It is a licensed premises. There is a wine bar adjacent to a snack bar and children under 18 usually sit in the snack bar and [are] bought drinks by friends who are 18 . . . She has admitted previously to drinking alcohol. I don't think she has her parents permission to go to the pool room. I have told her I don't think it is a good place to spend one's time. The answer I am usually given is that there is no where else to go in Blacktown. She gave no reason for being out to 12.30 on the time recently when she was spoken to by police. (Court Report, 25 October 1979)

Clearly, the focus of juvenile justice intervention had shifted in Terry's case from an initial concern with what she did at school to what she did outside school, particularly in her leisure time and in public places. This is significant because it occurred in twenty-one of the twenty-four cases where the schooling authorities initially channelled girls into the reaches of the juvenile justice authorities. Anny John's case further illustrates how this umbrella effect works.

Anny was originally committed to a juvenile detention centre for school default. Subsequent to this she was committed to detention a further three times for non-criminal conduct which had nothing to do with schooling. The justice authorities only became aware of this conduct because Anny had come to their attention through notification from the school authorities. The focus of scrutiny quickly shifted from her absences from school to her conduct outside school, as the Court Report quoted below suggests.

Anny first came under notice when she commenced truanting from school with her younger sister and spent much of her time with a girl aged 16 years who has since appeared before the court and released on probation. The girl has been associating with males and females much older than herself and over the past three weeks prior to her committal she had frequently left her home during the day and not returning until very late at night and sometimes early hours of the morning. She was first taken into custody on 20 January 1976 and remanded in custody when she was released on remand to her parents till her court appearance. She was attending X Public School and had just completed 5th class and was to go up to 6th class in 1977. Reports from the school have revealed that she has had rather a poor attitude and has been a behaviour problem within the school. (Court Report, 4 February, 1977)

Later that year, only six weeks after being released from custody,

Anny reappeared before the court in much the same way. Upon being committed the details of her offence were recorded as follows:

> Child had been truanting from school and had refused to go to school on some days. Child has constantly left home and has been returning late at nights. When asked where she had been the child refused to say. Child also left home on Sunday night and when asked who she went with, she refused to say. It was put to the child that from a medical report obtained, there was definite evidence that frequent intercourse had taken place and that the child admitted that she had had intercourse with about eight boys since being released from Ormond six weeks ago, but she refused to state any names or stated she did not know the boy's names. (Record of Case on Committal to an Institution, 14 October 1977)

For most girls whose cases involved truancy (forty-three in total) it seems that once identified as truants it was difficult for them *not* to get into further trouble with the justice authorities over matters totally unrelated to schooling. At the time of reading these cases my initial impression was to take them as indicative of the way in which schools routinely deal with female truants. This led me to conceive schools as being sites of social control—as extra-judicial agencies which manufacture female delinquency by providing the State with a fertile source of potential recruits to the female delinquent population. In what follows I assess the force of this initial impression and other related arguments about the way in which schools function in modern society as sites for the containment and control of errant youth.

Universal education and the social control of youth

Cases like the ones discussed above have led social theorists in Australia and other comparable countries, such as Britain and the United States, to see the emergence of universal education as a form of social control over the children of the working classes, the dispossessed and the poor because only their children seem to be affected (for example, Bowles and Gintis, 1970; Corrigan, 1979; Humphries, 1981; Johnson, 1976; Sharp, 1980; Willis, 1977). In this large body of literature schools are seen to: reproduce social and class inequality (Bowles and Gintis, 1970; Willis, 1983 p. 110); secure cultural dominance (Johnson, 1976, p. 50); sustain dominant class, race and gender relations (Sharp, 1980; White, 1990, pp. 77–8); and to prepare students ideologically for a social world riddled with injustice and inequality (Kenway, 1985, p. 139). It is also commonly argued in this literature that compulsory education arose in Western countries not from any benevolent concern to provide working-class children with an education, but out of a more important need to inure a whole class of children in the habits of order, restraint, discipline, thrift and sobriety—the qualities necessary for factory labour (Johnson, 1976, p. 46). Compulsory education was a sham which did little more than ameliorate the social problems of increasingly urbanised societies, such as juvenile delinquency, street gangs, vagrancy and idleness, by replacing idleness with the toil of discipline and industriousness (Johnson, 1976, p. 48).

Further support for this line of argument can be found in many of the arguments for compulsory mass education, philanthropic efforts and the extension of the apparatus of inspection (such as local health boards and local school boards) in the nineteenth century. Such measures appear to be conceived in broadly the same terms—as a need to overcome the legal obstacles in the way of a more thorough tutelary reach into the lives of the urban poor. The image of schools as sites for the transmission of moral technologies more concerned with qualities of obedience than with quality education appears to have a good deal of empirical substance, for example, a letter issued to State school teachers in 1867 by William Wilkins, Secretary of the Council of Education in NSW. The purpose of the document seems to be to inform teachers of the moral qualities that they were expected to inculcate in the classroom:

> The formation of habits of regularity, cleanliness, and orderly behaviour; the inculcation of regard for the rights of property, public and private; the growth of a spirit of obedience to the law, and respect for duly constituted authority; the correct practical appreciation of the value of time as an element of worldly success; the implanting of love for patient and sustained exertion in some industrial pursuit; and the development of a character for energy and self-reliance . . . Honesty, truthfulness, temperance and other virtues, may be cultivated by school discipline, reverence for sacred things may be fostered . . . a religious spirit may be educed [sic] by a teacher who exhibits in the performance of his own duty the prompting of religious influences. 1867 Circular, NSW Secretary Council of Education (*Source*: Barcan, 1980, p. 138)

A second document which argues explicitly for introducing compulsory education as a method of disciplining children is perhaps even more blunt. It is a record of the proceedings of a nineteenth century International Penitentiary Congress, the relevant extracts of which are quoted below:

> If we could provide criminal training without subjecting youths to the stigma of a criminal proceeding, we should do much good . . . By staying at school all day, they (children) were able to learn at

least the elements of civilisation and good manners, cleanliness and
so on, and that learning had its good effect upon their parents and
all with whom they came in contact. (Proceedings from the
International Penitentiary Congress, July 3–13, 1872).

And, referring to the role of reformatories, industrial schools, work-
house schools and compulsory education:

> . . . even these four agencies for ameliorating the condition of our
> neglected classes would leave a large area for philanthropic effort in
> our great towns. In order to be sent to a reformatory a child must
> have committed a distinct act, indicating the necessity for
> reformation; in order to be sent to an industrial school a child must
> be wholly neglected and likely to fall into crime; before entering a
> workhouse a child must be essentially a pauper . . . And many
> children who would emerge daily from homes in wretched alleys,
> cellars, and garrets, in which they would be subjected to the most
> dreadful influences; and looking to the morally pestiferous
> atmosphere breathed by many who would not come more under the
> influence of the law then, there was a very large field open to ladies
> and others for doing a great work in improving the parents of the
> children. (Proceedings of the International Penitentiary Congress,
> July 3–13, 1872)

My own experience of schooling confirms this portrait of schooling as a site for the transmission of moral qualities of dubious value
to students, such as submission to authority and an unquestioning
attitude to bodies of knowledge. Nevertheless, to see schools only
in negative terms as sites of social control leaves no possibility for
either a critical pedagogy or for a vision of schools as sites integral
to the formation of democratic and responsible citizens. Like a set
of Russian dolls, schools are conceived in these discourses as
miniature models of the original, over-arching structure of oppression (Donzelot, 1979). I now want to consider another way of taking
up these important issues about the role of education in the government of youth.

Universal education and citizenship

From the cases reviewed in this chapter it is obvious that educational
agencies are unavoidably embroiled in controlling and disciplining
youth and in enforcing their attendance at school. However, what
this means is not so obvious. One way of taking up the issue is to
argue that judicial and extra-judicial agencies acquire access to
clients and future recruits (both children and families) through the
surveillance of student populations provided by State educational
institutions. The implication of this is that schools have become part

of a matrix of normalising agencies which encircle the child and the family. This alliance has decentred decision-making processes and has given schools an important role in the process whereby decisions are made to call for judicial assistance in dealing with truants and other 'problem youth'. These decisions are then transported in space and time to the Children's Court via the admissibility of evidence which concentrates on the individual child, their background, family and schooling. In the majority of cases which end up in court, judicial logic, which focuses on the commission of an alleged offence, is marginalised by a focus on the individual. In this process, the commission of an offence, such as truancy, merely presents the occasion for conducting a wider inquiry to assess whether the child, and/or the child's family, needs normalising intervention and, if so, of what kind. Thus the strategic alliance between the schooling authorities and the agencies of juvenile justice which emerges in the criminalisation process can have 'the effect of extending the judicial further into the social via non-judicial means of penetration' (Burchell, 1979, p. 125). The initial detection as truant merely provides the opportunity for the disciplinary gaze of the justice authorities to extend their tutelary reach into the lives of errant youth, as it did in Terry's case, and the many others examined.

While not disagreeing with this scenario, or with the suggestion that schools are a crucial part of that great pedagogic effort directed at the government of youth, it must be acknowledged that the cases discussed above are by definition the ones in which the school authorities chose to seek judicial intervention. They represent only those cases dealt with through the courts and this is not the way that schools more routinely deal with truants and 'problem students' by referring to internal discipline procedures set out in specific school policies. It would therefore be mistaken to assume that schools always choose to deal with truants as they did in these cases. It is not known in how many cases schools choose to simply ignore truancy or to adopt a non-judicial course of action, such as putting a truant on detention or suspension. Consequently there are considerable disparities in how schools choose to administer sanctions and this is particularly the case with truancy (Slee, 1992, p. 22).

The notion that compulsory schooling has emerged simply as a capitalist imperative for reproducing exploitable labour, while not without empirical substance (some of which has been quoted above), is nevertheless open to challenge in two significant respects. First, the initiative for universal education came from a disparate array of sources, none of which included capitalists who, of course, wanted children to work in their factories and not attend school. Nor did the initiative for providing compulsory schooling come from the capitalist state. Its initiative came primarily from outside the state and its agencies and pre-dated any official state involvement. Those involved in establishing universal education in Britain included workers' guilds, churches, philanthropists (such as Hannah Moor, Wilberforce and the Hills sisters), journalists such as Henry Mayhew, and other odd organisations like the National Association for the Promotion of Social Science formed in Birmingham in 1857. Two philanthropic organisations in particular were instrumental in the establishment of a system of universal schooling in England. Both were church organisations. The National Society for the Provision of Education to the Poor was run by the Church of England and the British and Foreign Society was set up by the Methodist Church (Johnson, 1979, pp. 13–28). These organisations began operating a system of parish schools from the early 1830s. Trade unions and workers' guilds also had a tradition of providing education and literacy skills to their members well before compulsory schooling ever took shape. State involvement in schooling grew, usually by demands for funding school building projects, then by providing a school inspectorate and then through the institution of a system of teacher training. Legislation providing for the universal education of children was enacted in England in 1870 some forty years after the initiatives of these other bodies (Johnson, 1970, p. 117). It has even been suggested that 'the *Education Act* of 1870 was, for most English people, the first sensible impact of the administrative State on their private lives' (Young, 1965, p. 116). Ten years later NSW, then a colony of Britain, followed suit and enacted legislation providing for universal education. While this disparate set of philanthropists and charitable organisations cannot be said to have been the bearers of 'revolutionary' fervour, neither could they be accused of being apologetic about the untrammelled excesses of capitalism.

This leads me to a second major problem with simply seeing schools as forms of social control over the young. Universal education is a compulsory social obligation and not a matter of individual choice, but it also extends citizenship rights to youth. Any reasonable assessment of universal education must take into account the positive attributes which it confers on the young, such as literacy and protection from exploitation. It has to be remembered that a major concern both in Britain and the colonies at the time of the establishment of universal education was the employment of children for factory labour. The provision of universal education and the institution of legislation preventing the employment of children, were among the remedies suggested by charitable bodies to protect children from being exploited (Proceedings of the National

Association for the Promotion of Social Science, 1857, pp. xxviii). Only the crudest of interpretations could abstract from this a unitary logic of social control underlying the emergence of compulsory schooling both here and abroad.

It is not necessary to depict the institutions involved in providing universal education as benign or effective. But neither is it necessary to see in schools an extension of social control, the inevitable replication of the same logic which seeks to produce forms of conduct functional to the reproduction of patriarchy or capitalism. Schools are forms of government over youth which operate according to a limited grid of norms and regulations. They can be, or at least have the potential to be, places of critical pedagogy integral to the formation of responsible citizens, and they contribute to the revitalisation of a democratic public life by creating 'a public sphere of citizens who are able to exercise power over their own lives and especially over the conditions of knowledge production and acquisition' (Giroux, 1992, p. 47). The flip side to the control dimensions of universal education is the extension of citizenship rights to youth. Nicholas Rose puts it this way:

> Education was a personal right for the child irrespective of his or her parent's wishes, but it also recognised and imposed a social and collective right—the duty of each individual to improve and civilise themselves for the benefit of the social health of the community. (Rose, 1989, pp. 122)

I am not trying to depict the provision of universal education as entirely benign or satisfactory. Nor am I in any way endorsing the action of the justice authorities in taking truants into custody or the actions of particular school authorities in seeking justice intervention. I am not suggesting that their actions are simply misguided forms of benevolence. On the contrary, I would suggest that court action for truancy in the cases I examined did not arise from any benign concern to provide such girls with an education from which they could escape a domestic future or build a better life. The evidence of this is indisputable. In over half of the cases where girls were taken into custody for truancy they were sent to detention centres not equipped to provide educational instruction and from which they were released with school exemptions. This happened to both Sandra and Terry. In Terry's case the district officer who acted as the complainant recommended a committal to an institution because she 'felt that her best interests would be served by a period at Anglewood, as she would there get the necessary schooling' (Court Report, 21 September 1979). As there were no vacancies in any of the training schools for truants Terry was sent to a juvenile detention centre where no provision was made for educational training. Terry's mother lodged an appeal to the District Court on the grounds that the penalty imposed was too severe. The appeal was dismissed. Seven months later Terry was released from the detention centre with a school exemption. In releasing her the Superintendent of the institution outlined the following grounds for granting the exemption.

> Terry is not well motivated to return to school, and despite her assessed intelligence, due to lack of interest and concentration she performs poorly at school. Her mother has also requested that, because of poor financial circumstances, Terry be allowed to leave school and seek employment. This is also supported by the district office and would appear to be in her best interests. *Committee Recommendation*: to be discharged to parents with a school exemption (Recommendation For Release, 3 May 1979)

The argument that justice intervention was operating in any way in Terry's 'best interests' is farcical given that what was considered her best interests simply shifted to rationalise a variety of contradictory decisions made by the district officer, the detention centre and the Children's Court. Initially it was 'in her best interests' to be forced to attend school. The diametrically opposite course of action, to be given a school exemption, was then recommended as 'in her best interests'. To be sent to a Special School for Truants where Terry would have no choice but to attend school was initially regarded as in her 'best interests'. To be sent to a juvenile institution which made no provision for the education of inmates was, at a District Court level, ultimately sanctioned as being in Terry's 'best interests'. The reasons for Terry's committal to juvenile detention are quite transparent. Juvenile justice intervention in Terry's life was concerned more with subsidising an alleged 'lack of parental control' (Court Report), than with subsidising an inadequate education and her detection as a truant merely provided the welfare authorities with the means by which to remove her from her family. Clearly, girls like Terry and Sandra experienced futile and coercive forms of juvenile justice intervention which did nothing to enhance their future prospects in life and probably a lot to damage them.

The management of truancy through juvenile justice is inconsistent with the pedagogic objective of producing responsible citizens. It therefore makes sense that schools *should* strive to insulate girls like Terry and Sandra from the clutches of the justice authorities and most probably do. The criticism of the schools attended by the girls whose cases have been discussed in this chapter is why these schools chose to surrender the government of children under their tutelage to the justice authorities. Social responsibility is the flip side of universal education. These schools failed in their social duty to adequately provide a positive educational environment for girls like Sandra and Terry. Making truancy an offence provides the schooling authorities with a direct path for dumping their 'management problems' at the door of the juvenile justice agencies. This is what is so particularly disturbing about the recent educational 'reforms'.

5 Policing the families of delinquent girls

> The Department strongly believes in the importance of the preventative work done by its field officers with young people and their families, when their pattern of behaviour brings them to the notice of the community . . . Casework with families in which the parents seem unable to cope adequately is given primary importance, for it is from these problem families that many instances of anti-social behaviour arise. (NSW Child Welfare Department, *Annual Report*, 1969, p. 11)

At first it may seem rather odd to claim that delinquent girls are *not* the main or sole focus of juvenile justice intervention. Much of the field work carried out by the juvenile justice agencies is actually directed at families, siblings and kin relations in ways which are far from trivial or accidental as the passage above indicates. These specific forms of intervention use the 'predelinquent girl' as a route to the 'problem family'. When this occurs, juvenile justice functions as little more than a moralising device to gain access to those marginalised families whose conduct digresses from the cultural specificity of normative expectations about family life. This intervention is far from being either satisfactory or benign. There was an abundance of such intervention documented in the cases in this study.

Juvenile justice intervention also punishes children, especially girls, for the failures and abuses of their parents, particularly in cases of sexual abuse. The abused child is subsumed into the discourses about problem children or predelinquent youth and drawn into the same forms of discipline as young offenders simply for having been abused. This is what I refer to as the welfare/justice nexus which gives rise to a serious and debilitating dilemma. Clearly, the justice authorities have a responsibility to intervene into abusive families to pursue the important social objective of protecting children. However, in some cases (Judy's, for example) this responsibility is often thwarted and in others simply provides the pretext for a repressive moralising device which punishes the 'dysfunctional' family by removing its 'predelinquent' children. The 'problem' family comes to be policed through a governmental apparatus which both restrains and protects the rights of the child through a disciplinary regime of departmental supervision. In vital respects this dilemma can be seen to be weaving through most of the cases already considered and is the focus of specific attention in this chapter. It is a dilemma which has connections with therapeutic familialism (Burchell, 1980), a practice which takes a highly fictionalised image of the nuclear family as a gauge from which to measure, model and re-model almost every form of social arrangement, including juvenile justice institutions and State ward shelters.

Supervising families

Families who come to the notice of authorities *and* who are assessed as dysfunctional come under a system of what the department calls 'preventative family supervision'. The main purpose of this supervision is to manage the effects of some departmentally defined family pathology. Not all of this supervision is court-ordered. Information about the extent of preventative family supervision is patchy, but what statistics exist in relation to this matter suggest that most family casework is, in fact, *not* court-ordered.[1]

Donzelot refers to this particular strategy of managing the 'problem' family as a form of tutelage: 'In essence, tutelage means that these families will be stripped of all effective rights and brought into a relation of dependence vis-a-vis welfare and educative agents' (Donzelot, 1979, p. xxi). In a formal legal sense, families under tutelage have their parental rights in relation to their children replaced by that of the State. In New South Wales, the Minister of the department is actually considered to be the legal guardian of every State ward that comes into State care. This authority is then delegated to the discretion of a range of social workers and other educative and medical agents. One obvious problem with this system of tutelage is that those with the least accountability exercise the most power. District officers, child protection workers, social workers, psychologists, probation officers, young offender support workers, school counsellors and, to some extent, school teachers, baby health sisters and health care professionals are the primary bearers of this discretion. It is they who will decide which families should be diverted from the court process and continue to be supervised and which will be punished by having their children removed. Indeed, the underlying rationale of preventative supervision, as the passage below indicates, is to normalise clients without having to resort to court action.

Preventative measures taken by the department result in many behaviour problems being resolved without the necessity for court action. (NSW Child and Social Welfare Department, 1970, pp. 19–21)

Punishment or court action is usually considered as a last resort for those families who continue to disregard the advice of the experts or who fail to adjust in ways the department considers appropriate. The families whose case histories are discussed in this chapter are examples of this latter group.

The families in this case history sample had been under departmental supervision for an average of nine years. Some of their children were even born under supervision. More than half of the 370 children among the fifty-nine families in this sample had appeared before the Children's Court including the fifty-nine delinquent girls from the case history sample. One third had been made State wards and one fifth had been committed to juvenile detention centres. The cohort of families experienced high unemployment[2] and welfare dependency rates[3], at 37.5 per cent and 43 per cent respectively. One third of the families were single-parent, compared with the Australian average of 7 per cent (*Australian Families* 1982, ABS Catalogue No. 4408.0). The average number of children in the families under supervision was six, compared with an Australian average of two (*Social Indicators* 1980, ABS, Catalogue No. 4101.0). There were very few home owners among these families, most were tenants,[4] and housing commission tenants in particular.[5] Of the few parents who were employed, most worked in the secondary labour market in low-paid intermittent jobs. Not surprisingly these families resided in two main socio-geographical districts—those generally considered to be working-class and those with a very high proportion of Aboriginal residents (Tables 2.1 and 3.2).

It is evident from this description that, of the families who come under departmental supervision, those that are taken to court are drawn from the most marginalised and welfare dependent sections of the population. How this happens, and the consequences of this for the family when it does happen, can be more clearly understood if a specific case where this has occurred is examined.

Christine's family

Christine was twelve years old when she was committed to State wardship on a charge of public mischief along with three younger siblings. Court documents described the incident in the following terms:

Christine with her two sisters and a brother went to the police with
a story that their younger sister had been sexually assaulted and
abducted. After a wide police search a man who fitted the
description of the man the Neaves' children told the Police was
arrested and taken to X Police Station. He was a prominent
businessman in Parramatta. After many interviews it was learnt that
the children had made up the story. (Court Officer's Report to
Establishments, 13 March 1976)

The case against the Neaves children did not rest on substantiat-
ing before the court that they were delinquent or that the family
was fraught with violence and conflict. In fact the department was
aware of a strong bond of affection between the children and their
parents and the court was even told that this was so. Rather, the
substance of the case against the Neaves children rested on expert
advice that the parents were incompetent and that the family was
dysfunctional. Initially that advice came from the supervising district officer. After describing details of both parents and thirteen
children the district officer provided the court with the following
lengthy report based on her inquiry into this family's background.

Home: The home is an old weatherboard cottage in a dilapidated
condition. It must be pointed out that the material conditions of the
home must now surely be better than any other home of the family.
Nevertheless the home is somewhat of a landmark in the area. In
comparison with the general standard it is well below par. The home
is rented and is to be demolished in the near future to make way for
a new shopping complex.
Income: Mr Neaves—Unemployed $86 per week.
           Board from four children $30 per week
Disbursements: Rent—$28 per week
This family has always been in financial difficulties.
General: This family has been supervised by the Department on a
preventative basis since 1962 when a complaint of neglect and poor
school attendance was received. Since that time the family have
moved on numerous occasions always to run-down homes and
always where the children have not had adequate bedding. Over the
years Mr Neaves has had numerous jobs, mainly as a truck driver,
but interspersed with periods of unemployment. This man has been
unemployed since July 1974 and to my mind has made no concerted
effort to obtain a position to support his family. The family has
always been in financial difficulty and all major voluntary agencies
have been involved until they have withdrawn, stating they were not
prepared to help the family any longer.
    All of the older children have appeared before the Court on
different complaints. Sara ran away from home and was committed
to an institution. Fred was charged with indecently assaulting a
young girl. Vicki and Matthew, school defaulters, ran away from
home and were committed to an institution. Paul has been on

probation. Debbie was also committed to an institution as she would not remain in the home and is currently on probation. This lass is currently residing at a halfway house and was a police witness in a carnal knowledge matter two weeks ago. To my mind this girl is the 'scapegoat' of the family and is blamed for many arguments that occur in the home. Heather is a restored ward and is also currently on probation for running away from home. This is Roger's first court appearance. This is also the first court appearance for Christine and Lynnette.

This family requires close supervision. The one redeeming factor being that there is a reasonably warm, dependent relationship between the parents and younger children. Both Mr and Mrs Neaves have recently joined the Bowling Club and are spending some time away from home. They state that they cannot understand why their children behave the way they do because they have given them everything and try to be good parents. Because of their limited intelligence and response to critical advice family casework is somewhat limited. Mr Neaves' comment to me regarding the children's criminal offence was that he could see no serious consequences other than the fact that the police had been embarrassed about it. He cannot see that there are serious problems underlying his children's act, and again this limits counselling. Further disturbing [sic] is the fact that these young children appear to be fully aware of sexual terms and actions, and while there is no concrete evidence regarding any type of sexual misconduct there still exists a niggling doubt. The only evidence there has been during my supervision is a reported assault on one of the girls by the older brother, towards the end of last year. There was no medical evidence to substantiate this.

I strongly feel that Mr and Mrs Neaves could make a concerted effort to give the proper control and care to their children and that Mr Neaves could make every effort to obtain a job so that his example can be beneficial to his children with regard to taking his place in the community. Over the years it has been considered that these parents are borderline incompetent and close supervision has been given, although without much improvement in the standard of living and care of the children, but because of the bond between the children and parent it is considered that Christine should be returned to the care of her parents for a probationary period. This is the first time the lass has appeared before a Children's Court. She admits writing obscene letters with the intention of incriminating her older sister. This action was in collaboration with another sister. Christine enters High School this year and it is hoped she will be placed in the normal streams as it appears she is brighter than the other children. I have always found her to be co-operative reliable and pleasant. However, the inevitable personal disintegration within this family has commenced in relation to Christine. It is hoped that this Court appearance has had a beneficial effect on the lass and that

close supervision will assist the lass to cope within her family unit
to which she is warmly attached. (Court Report, 4 March 1976)

Prior to the court appearance both parents and children were sent
to a Child Guidance Clinic for assessment. The psychologist who
undertook that assessment provided the following advice to the court
about the 'incompetent parental management' of Christine's family.

The above named four children were interviewed and tested in this
Clinic on the 3rd March 1976. Their parents attended for assessment
on 29 February 1976. It was established that an older child of the
family was fully assessed here in June 1974 following a charge of
uncontrollable. She is at present completely rejected by the family
and lives elsewhere. Both Mr and Mrs Neaves present as
intellectually dull and insightless. It was no use trying to gain
comprehensive material regarding the family's daily functioning, as
they were unable to perceive that there was a problem at all or to
speculate about the causal factors in their children's offensive
behaviour. It is, however, abundantly clear that the major part of the
Neaves' children's problem behaviour has its roots in incompetent
parental management, due to specific parental inadequacy. This is a
multi-problem family known to and supported by the department of
YACS for twelve years. Behaving in a manner unacceptable to
broader society to the children merely means conforming to the
closest values and norms they know i.e. those held by
subcultural-type family unit. On testing the Children intellectually,
the following results were indicated.
1st Child—low average
2nd Child—low average
3rd Child—upper average
4th Child—mentally retarded
Their scholastic performance is consistent with this finding. No
evidence of serious mental illness was found in any of these four
children. They are considered to be emotionally, intellectually and
socially deprived. They are four of ten illegitimate children to their
parents who have 18 children between them, eight from former
unions. I see no easy solution. The prognosis for rehabilitation of
the family as a whole is considered poor. The likelihood of them
remaining a community liability for a long while to come, is fairly
strong . . . Eventual environmental manipulation of these children
seems inevitable. (Psychological Assessment for Children's Court, 4
March 1976)

Despite the fact that the district officer recommended a period
of probation the presiding magistrate committed three of the four
children before the court, including Christine, to wardship. The older
sibling involved in the prank was sentenced to a juvenile detention
centre. Soon after her committal a report on Christine's file stated
the she 'was most upset at being made a State ward—the separation

from her family has distressed her greatly' (Assessment Report on Ward, 13 March 1976).

The permanent removal of the Neaves children through their committal to State wardship was considered necessary not so much because of the nature of the offence, but because of the nature of the family. The Neaves were considered 'a multi-problem family' known to the department for twelve years. The family had been under departmental supervision even before Christine was born. Christine was one of ten children living in the home, but had another seven siblings living elsewhere. All her older siblings had appeared before the Children's Court for one reason or another, but most for school default. The parents were assessed as 'culturally deprived', 'intellectually dull and insightless', 'borderline incompetent' and 'lacking control over their children'. Not only did the parents refuse to accept the advice of the experts but they apparently asserted the legitimacy of a different set of family values and resisted the intrusions of the welfare. It was this evidence of an oppositional family culture about which the child welfare agencies expressed much fear, frustration and anger. In the view of the child welfare authorities, the Neaves were the kind of family who reared delinquents, louts and unemployables, not law-abiding citizens. It was not the kind of family through which State agencies could exercise governance—through adherence to contemporary educative, medical and legal norms. The Neaves were considered to be a 'community liability' and neither the school nor the welfare agencies could exert any moral authority over this family to make them 'better citizens'.

As with many cases of alleged or reported child abuse (Carter *et al.*, 1988, p. 22) poverty has, in this case, become synonymous with parental incompetence. Not surprisingly 'the effects of such a strategy have fallen predominantly on the working-class family' (Collison, 1980, p. 158). Once assessed as incompetent, the basis exists, as Donzelot suggests, for the liberal state to dispense with consent, appropriating the children and eschewing the family's parental rights. This is exactly what happened to Mr and Mrs Neaves. They were classified as dysfunctional and their children were appropriated into State care. The department was so zealous about keeping the children out of contact with their parents—requests for weekend and holiday leave with their children were continually refused. Reasons given for denying the parents' request for weekend leave usually took the following form.

Miss X the district officer feels that weekend leave should not be granted for Christine as yet. This is part of the incentive for the

Neaves family to seriously attempt to establish an acceptable
standard. (Note on file, Placement Officer, 25 May 1976)

An observation about the history of juvenile justice mechanisms
in another Australian State succinctly describes the disciplinary
process in which the Neaves family was enmeshed.

It is not so much the bold, threatening child who is in need of
reform as the undisciplined family who need to be regulated and
shown the correct attitudes or their children will be appropriated.
(Tyler, 1983, p. 10)

Here, we most clearly see the dilemma posed by the policing of
families through forms of government which use children as the
vehicle for the normalisation of parents. The protection of children
operates through their own restraint. Another paradox then emerges.
The children of this family were to be saved from 'inevitable
disintegration' initially through departmental supervision, then
through their appropriation as State wards. Disintegrate they did.
After being made a State ward and taken into protective custody,
Christine reappeared before the court a further three times and
eventually found herself in a juvenile detention centre. This is the
fate of so many State wards who, once drawn into the welfare
system, are pulled into the orbit of the juvenile justice agencies and
later, as adults, into the reaches of the criminal justice agencies.

The main conclusion to be drawn from Christine's case is that
decisions about what to do with a child before the Children's Court
rest heavily upon the character of the child's family, as supplied to
the court by various experts, and not as commonly believed, on
events surrounding the commission of a discrete act or crime. The
juvenile justice authorities regard the family as both the source and
saviour of juvenile delinquency. The family of the delinquent child
is thus held to account for the deviance of its members, just as Mrs
and Mr Neaves were held responsible for the petty misdemeanours
of their children. The emphasis on parental responsibility is
becoming more apparent in the current political context. Parents
whose children are convicted of crimes are being required to pay
the court costs, fines and other penalties (*Sydney Morning Herald*,
22 February, 1990) and parents can now be fined for not sending
their children to school. If families fail to normalise their children's
delinquencies (or predelinquencies) their parental rights may be
removed and their children taken into custody as wards or as
institutional inmates. Because the family is internally differentiated
according to age and sex it is mothers who bear the chief
responsibility for the conduct of their children—as well as the
consequences of their misconduct. This issue is taken up in more

detail below through the case history of another girl, whom I have called Kathy.

Punishing mothers

It should be clear from the above that juvenile justice intervention can be used as a means to exercise leverage over the 'problem family'. Within the family, the mother is often singled out as the vehicle for the diffusion of socially acceptable norms of conduct. This is why 'bad' mothers are often held responsible for the delinquencies of their children. They are considered to have failed to fulfil a civic duty of immense importance—the proper care and government of their children. 'Bad mothering' thus provides 'the welfare' with all the rationale needed for 'preventative intervention' and ultimately for the appropriation of children into State care if that intervention fails to bring about the required adjustments in family life. While Kathy Jones' case bears out many of the themes already discussed in relation to Christine's case, it adds an important dimension to an analysis of the methods used to police families and govern children, through the punishment of mothers.

Kathy's notes

Kathy appeared before the Children's Court five times between the ages of twelve and fifteen years; three times for being uncontrollable and twice for absconding from a ward establishment. She was one of eight children, six of whom were living in the family home (a standard three-bedroom fibro housing commission dwelling). The family had undergone many years of financial hardship as paid work for both parents was interspersed with lengthy periods of illness and unemployment. The family had also been under departmental supervision since 1962, the year Kathy was born. During that year an older sister, then aged twelve, was a victim of sexual assault. Departmental supervision was requested by the magistrate 'who commented adversely on the lack of parental control and poor environment at that time' (Application for Restoration, 4 February 1974). A note pinned to the front page of Kathy's dossier depicts quite succinctly the image of the family portrayed within its many pages.

> Spoke to regular district officer (who) said the family were hopeless—had been under casework supervision since 1962—parents were irresponsible and ineffectual and their lives revolve around the hotel—they didn't care much about the children. Most of the older children have been in institutions and haven't done well. (Note on File, 25 January 1976)

Kathy was born into a status of supervision—a status which meant that she and her siblings were under constant scrutiny by 'the welfare'. In fact the same district officer had supervised the family since 1965. Four of Kathy's older siblings had been before the Children's Court at one time or another, mostly for welfare related complaints and this is how Kathy's behaviour first came to the notice of the authorities. It was the district officer who, during a routine home visit probation check of an older sister, initiated court action against Kathy and her two younger brothers. All three children were charged with being uncontrollable, taken to court and made State wards. They were kept in a remand centre in Sydney for a short time before being split up. Kathy was sent to a departmental shelter for girls in Sydney. Her brothers were sent to a ward establishment outside Sydney. Both establishments were hundreds of kilometres from the district where they had lived, making it immensely difficult for their parents to make regular visits. The parents requested the immediate return of their children. In a burst of anger Mrs Jones confronted the district officer insisting that her children had done nothing wrong and should not have been taken away from her. The district officer's report, quoted below, strenuously denies this claim and recommends that the children remain in departmental care.

The Home: Three bedroom housing commission dwelling
fibro/cement construction.
Financial Position: As both parents work the family should be in a
satisfactory financial position but I understand this is not the case as
both are heavy drinkers.
General: The history of the family is well documented as they have
been under supervision since 1962, when the eldest daughter then
aged 12 was the victim of a sexual assault when left by her parents
who were drinking at the local hotel. The case was originally drawn
to the department's attention by Justice X who commented adversely
on the lack of parental control and poor environment at that time. I
personally have visited this family since 1965. During that time
there has been a sad story of lack of parental interest and control
with the children starting a familiar pattern of school default in
primary school and drifting on to predelinquent activities early in
High School and eventually appearing before the local Children's
Court. Vickie, John and Lisa have all appeared before the local
Children's Court. Sandra is currently on probation as the result of
an appearance before Court in February 1974. She in not attending
school at the moment although of school age.
     The subject children were committed to wardship after a long
series of truancy episodes of up to a week, it is significant that
rarely were these absences reported to this department or to the
local police. Apparently the parents were not concerned about their

children or did not wish to draw further attention to themselves. The parents demand the return of their children, but have little insight into the long standing problems which led to their committal. Their pattern of living is the same as formerly and they cannot perceive that the children's difficulties are largely due to a negative disinterested attitude by the parents. I am convinced that should the subject children be returned to their parents they would follow in the footsteps of the older siblings within a short time. In my view the children would be much better off in the care of the department. *Recommendation*: decline application for restoration. (Application for Restoration, 4 February 1975)

After being made a State ward Kathy remained in a distressed state—she was wrenched from all family ties, including contact with her brothers who were also made State wards. She made two attempts to abscond from the ward shelter and several to take her own life. Each time she tried to return home. Showing absolutely no leniency, on both occasions Kathy was charged with absconding[6] and, on the second occasion, was sentenced to a detention centre. Kathy spent seven months in detention before being released to her parents. Her release was delayed by several months because the district officer would not approve the home conditions as suitable for her return. It was only when her father was admitted to hospital with a terminal illness that approval was finally granted for Kathy to return home. Mr Jones died later that year.

Several months passed during which the district officer left the grieving family alone. However, almost immediately after the death of Mr Jones the district officer made another round of complaints against the children. The court dismissed the first of these. This is significant in itself. It says a lot about the zealousness of this district officer, given that the children's court rarely dismisses complaints unless they are withdrawn by the department. In this instance the presiding magistrate decided against the recommendation of the department. A couple of weeks later the supervising district officer tried again. This time charging Kathy with being uncontrollable, he claimed that she had stayed out at night without *his* knowledge and had not been of good behaviour. This time Kathy was not so lucky. The presiding magistrate concurred with the district officer's allegations and sent her to a detention centre.

Two months into her second committal, the district officer sent a report to the superintendent recommending that there was 'no possibility of returning home' (Home Report on Institutional Inmate, 6 February 1976). Singling out the mother the district officer stated:

I feel that I could still not recommend that Kathy return to her home because Mrs Jones shows little control and little apparent concern for the girl. She was only restored a period of just over three months [ago] and in that time had two court appearances for uncontrollability. On both occasions Mrs Jones had not bothered to contact me immediately or inform the police of the fact that the girl is missing. Kathy has many friends in the area but unfortunately most of them are unfavourably known and I feel that if she were returned to her mother it would be only a short period before she transgressed again. *Recommend*: no possibility of returning home (Home Report on Institutional Inmate, 6 February 1976)

With a view to releasing Kathy, the superintendent requested another home report and received the following all too predictable reply which amounted to little more than a character assassination of each family member residing in the home.

At the present time, Anne, Mrs Jones' married daughter, is residing in the home. She is separated from her husband and his whereabouts are unknown. Her three children are wards and I believe that they are placed in foster homes. Anne's reputation since going to the Jones' home has been most unsatisfactory. She is visiting numerous hotels and apparently becoming under the influence of intoxicating liquor. She is also gaining another reputation but I do not feel competent to comment on this. It has been suggested to Anne that she should attempt to stay at home and save her money in the hope that she may be able to re-establish herself, obtain a home and apply for restoration of her children. At present she is in receipt of unemployment benefits and pays Mrs Jones about $6.00 per week. The rest she uses on her own activities.

Sandra is a bit disgruntled at home. She is talking of leaving and going to live with her sister Anne. Sandra has applied for unemployment benefits and it seems fairly certain that these will be granted. If it is granted she claims that she will pay probably about $3 or $4 per week board to her mother. It was suggested to Sandra that this was not sufficient under the girl's circumstances if she obtains $31 per week.

It has also been recently discovered that Mrs Jones was admitted to hospital some two to three months ago. She had been out drinking with some of her companions and it was necessary to admit her for medical treatment. She was detained at the hospital overnight. From all reports her behaviour, condition and actions in the hospital were deplorable. Mrs Jones has been extensively questioned regarding this and said that she only went out to have a couple of drinks with her friends. Mrs Jones was also recently seen at the TAB [betting office] and for a woman with such little means she is apparently not doing too badly for herself. Mrs Jones could give no reasonable explanation for going to the hotel or the TAB but said that she feels she needs some form of recreation and she needs friends.

It will be noted of course that previously when Kathy was restored on both known occasions that Kathy left the home, Mrs Jones did not report the matter to the Department or the Police. In fact it was on both occasions that I had to ascertain the situation by visiting the family home. It has been pointed out to Mrs Jones that this totally irresponsible attitude is just not good enough and under the circumstances I would most certainly not support that Kathy or her brothers come home. I pointed out to Mrs Jones at length that the children could get themselves into any trouble and Mrs Jones would not even apparently attempt to contact the Department . . .

Obviously Mrs Jones is fairly well attached to her children but apparently is not prepared to be truthful, straightforward or in fact fair to the children by making a genuine effort to visit them. Mrs Jones has applied for restoration of the children. In view of the above I certainly could not recommend that (the children) be discharged to her care and I feel that I could not even recommend that the children come home for school holidays. This is simply because I cannot trust Mrs Jones I do not know of her behaviour and activities outside the home except if they are ascertained from somebody else. Local inquiries reveal that Kathy may have stayed away from home on at least two other occasions but the matter was not reported to the department. Strongly recommend that restoration of children be declined and that discharge of Kathy to mother be declined. (Home Report, 24 March 1975)

In desperation the superintendent made another futile request for Kathy to be allowed to return home. Kathy had now over-stayed the duration of her sentence in a detention centre. Not surprisingly the response from the district officer had not shifted.

Mrs Jones was a little upset at the time of visit as she had been sure that her children were coming home for the school holidays. I informed Mrs Jones that she could not be trusted to inform the department if there were any problems. I pointed out the fact to her that Kathy has left home on two occasions and at least remained out overnight and she had not informed me. Mrs Jones said that her children had done nothing wrong and should not be in homes. I feel that if the children were returned to her care and got into any sort of trouble or failed to go to school she would protect them, or just do nothing about it, as she did in the case of Kathy. Mrs Jones is a very difficult pathetic woman to encourage and could be described as being pathetic in general motivation. I feel that if the children were returned to her at the present time it would not be very long before they were in trouble . . . I am adamant that if the children are returned to her care it will not be very long before they are in conflict with the law. *Recommendation*: note that mother's circumstances are unchanged and that she has little motivation. (Home Report on Institution Inmate, 28 May 1976)

Kathy was never granted the required departmental approval to return home. Eventually the superintendent 'went around' the district officer, releasing Kathy into the care of another family, from which she made her way back to her own family—unbeknown to the supervising district officer. Little more is known about Kathy's movements after this as the family moved, not informing the department of their relocation, and the case notes stopped.

One of the most remarkable aspects of this case is that Mrs Jones was the primary target of the court action against her children. Taking her children to court as welfare cases provided the means through which she was continually punished for being what welfare officials thought was a 'bad' mother. Most of the evidence against Mrs Jones was of a moralistic nature describing her as 'pathetic', 'deplorable', 'lacking in motivation', 'untrustworthy' and 'deprived.' Much of the district officer's negative assessments of her arose simply because she refused to comply with his wishes and instructions—most of which were contrary to the best interests of her children. Mrs Jones protected her children from the intrusions of the welfare and because of this she was considered incapable of carrying out the civic responsibilities of motherhood. She failed to govern her children in socially acceptable ways by allowing them 'too much freedom', 'to stay out overnight' and to 'stay away from school'. She was 'immoral' because she went to the TAB and occasionally to the hotel. She was recalcitrant because she could not see any problem with her children, her mothering, going to the TAB or the way the family lived. Mrs Jones was also accused of producing a family of delinquent children. The main reason for refusing the restoration of the children to her care was the fear that they 'would come into conflict with the law'. In fact, over the eighteen-year period covered by these documents there is no evidence whatsoever that any of her eight children were convicted of a criminal offence. They were all taken to court as welfare cases, not juvenile offenders. The most serious charge for which any of her children appeared before the court was for being uncontrollable and the most serious misconduct was truanting from school or staying out overnight without telling the dreaded district officer! Hardly a family of delinquents!

No evidence was ever presented to the court that Mrs Jones physically or emotionally abused her children. In fact, the documentation about this in Kathy's notes supports the opposite view— that the family was a warm and loving one. Kathy certainly thought so. She told the social worker at the detention centre that 'her parents are good—has no complaints about home' and that she 'gets on really well with brothers and sisters and especially the brothers who were also made wards at the same time as Kathy' (Report on Institution Inmate, 2 January 1975). The psychologist who assessed her while in custody commented that 'Kathy became upset when her parents and family were discussed . . . she is obviously missing her family a great deal' (Psychological

Assessment, 25 January 1975). There is a glaring discrepancy between Kathy's regard for her family and the department's.

Clearly, juvenile justice has operated in this case as little more than a moralising device to punish a 'bad' mother to the great detriment of her children, particularly Kathy. As Christine had done, Kathy wound up in a detention centre as a result of attempting to return to a family from whom the department should never have taken her. Although preventative departmental supervision can rescue children from abusive family environments it can also bring the children of families like Kathy's and Christine's into a disciplinary gaze—a web of supervision which manufactures female delinquency by bringing the petty mundane conduct of such girls under intense and often zealous forms of scrutiny and control. Both girls were caught in the dilemma of being 'saved' through a supervisory mechanism of simultaneous protection and penality—of being 'liberated' from an officially classified dysfunctional family through the denial of their own liberty. These girls had no choice or say in whether they wanted to be committed to State care and little control over the events which pushed them along the fast track from care to detention. This dilemma has significant consequences for the politics of 'saving children'.

Saving children?

The main reason that children enter into either State wardship or substitute care seems to be poverty rather than child abuse, sexual abuse or unwillingness on the part of parents to provide (Sweeney, 1989, p. 305). In 1984, there were 24 250 children in Australia under State guardianship (Report of the Senate Standing Committee on Social Welfare, 1985, p. 43). Of these, somewhere between 7000 and 11 000 were in institutional care. Children under State guardianship represent less than 1 per cent of the population of children in Australia. Yet one in five State wards from the random sample of 1046 girls whose criminal records I studied ended up in a detention centre sometime during their adolescence. Using the same data, this compares with an average of less than one in 1000 for girls who are not State wards. Of the fifty-nine case studies, thirty-six cases were State wards—the vast majority of whom were made wards well before they were officially classified as young offenders. As State wards these girls were then drawn into a spiral of being committed to more disciplinary institutions for the most petty misbehaviour.

State wards are clearly an over-represented group in the young offender population. How this occurs through the nexus that exists between welfare and justice is explained more fully in the concluding chapter. The point relevant to the discussion here is that girls like Judy and Christine can hardly be said to have been 'saved' when, in fact, after being taken into the protective custody of the child welfare authorities they end up either in juvenile detention centres or in ward establishments run like detention centres.

There has been a recent chorus of condemnations about the treatment of State wards. One of the most significant voices has been that of Brian Burdekin the Human Rights Commissioner who has accused State governments of being grossly negligent in caring for their wards (*The Sydney Morning Herald*, 14 November 1988). Two other bodies, The Brotherhood of St Lawrence and Family Action, have joined the Human Rights and Equal Opportunity Commission in condemning State governments of being neglectful guardians pointing to a high rate of homelessness among State wards (*The Sydney Morning Herald*, 12 December 1990). The Youth Accommodation Association has also criticised the State government's handling of wards who now constitute one in five homeless youth seeking accommodation in New South Wales (*The Sydney Morning Herald*, 25 February 1991).

Clearly the child-saving efforts directed at girls like Terese, Kathy and Christine, far from being benevolent, have had disastrous effects on their lives. As wards they were sent to institutions steeped in stigma, surrounded by razor wire fences and treated like delinquents, being prevented from having contact with siblings, parents or friends. They had to wear government issue clothing, put up with the brutality of barrack living and somehow bear the intrusion of the welfare agencies into the most private aspects of their lives: their menstrual cycles were recorded and their mail was checked—some of it even being confiscated (Carrington, 1989, pp. 342–4). Some small comfort can be gained from the fact that during the last decade the shift in emphasis in child welfare policy in NSW from controlling uncontrollables to child protection has reduced the prospect that families like Christine's will come under preventative supervision. The drop in the average age at which juveniles have been appearing before the Children's Court for welfare matters during the last ten years confirms this trend.[7] Complacency about the current child welfare system is, however, premature as the shift toward child protection policies has given rise to a plethora of other problems associated with the politics of saving children.

The mandatory reporting of child abuse has been the major practical outcome of this shift toward child protection policies. In 1985, a child protection unit was established within the department to carry out this function as announced in the following extract from its *Annual Report*:

The Government's commitment to minimise the incidence and maximise the detection of child abuse and neglect has been reflected in new practices and programmes. New South Wales has become widely recognised as the most progressive service provider in this most vital area of responsibility. (Annual Report, 1985, p. 1)

Several years later, Virginia Chadwick, the then Minister for Family And Community Services (FACS), in publicising the apparent success of mandatory reporting released a departmental report which purported to show that 'Children who live in the poorest areas of metropolitan Sydney are eleven times more likely to suffer physical abuse than those in affluent areas' (*Sydney Morning Herald*, 27 October 1989). The figures were based on notifications of child abuse to the department by its agencies—agencies which just happen to be concentrated in the poorest areas of Sydney. There are other reasons for being sceptical about the validity of these figures and their interpretation by the then Minister. First, more than 50 per cent of reported cases are unsubstantiated (Carter, *et al.*, 1988, p. 28). Second, given that only a small proportion of notified cases of child abuse actually involve physical harm or sexual abuse most cases of neglect turn out to be synonymous with poverty as they did in the cases discussed previously. Third, the results contradict the findings of other studies which suggest that child abuse and incest are not necessarily confined to either the lower socio-economic classes or Aboriginal communities (Waldby, 1985).

Notifications of child abuse are neither an accurate nor reliable measure of its actual incidence, but they do suggest a great deal about the mechanisms set up to police child abuse. Because it is assumed that dysfunctional families give rise to juvenile delinquency, normalising agencies aim their interventions at a small residue of families in officially classified crime-prone or troublesome neighbourhoods in anticipation that this is where such families reside. Families living in these areas are then linked to a range of governmental apparatuses for supervising family life, through schools, baby health centres, public housing agencies, social security offices, public health centres and so on. I am not suggesting that all such programs are part of an over-arching form of social control involved in the generalised surveillance of socially disadvantaged communities, but I am suggesting that specific families within these communities are identified as targets for their operations. Once identified these particular families then become routinely subject to suspicion and surveillance of various kinds (Hogg and Golder, 1987, p. 67).

A more general problem with the mandatory reporting of child abuse is that it concentrates public resources in the notification process, shifting resources away from other much more positive kinds of family support, such as child care, after-school programs, rental assistance and so on. Nor does mandatory reporting offer any solutions to the complex problem of child abuse where such abuse is substantiated and does amount to serious harm. The notification process is simply a policing exercise which can neither deal with all cases notified nor offer any genuine assistance to families who need it. Of particular concern, is that by being steeped in stigma and punitiveness the policy may have the contrary effect of discouraging the demand for assistance where it is most needed—in real cases of incest and other kinds of child abuse. It is not difficult to see why a mother may fail to seek outside intervention if she fears it may result in considerable stigmatisation of herself and her children by doing so! Nor is it difficult to understand why girls like Judy will avoid going to the authorities with allegations of sexual abuse when they have good reason to fear that suspicion will turn attention to own their sexual conduct.

Government of and through the family

The cases discussed in this chapter point to an urgent need to rethink the social administration of family pathology through mechanisms of court-ordered family supervision and the committal of children to State wardship. Not only do such mechanisms offer little more than the opportunity for authorised family technicians to moralise about 'bad' families, but they do little to actually assist children genuinely in need of saving from abusive family environments. I would suggest that children whose families are genuinely abusive need positive alternatives to the family, such as long-term youth accommodation, rather than punitive solutions such as State ward institutions. They also need secure and adequate sources of income support. Child protection policies such as the mandatory notification of child abuse and the committal of abused children to State wardship currently do not offer, nor are they ever likely to offer, youth support programs and policies of a *positive* nature.

I am not suggesting a policy of radical non-intervention in family life. The family is neither an object, an enclosed institution, nor a receptacle for state intervention from without. The family is neither a boundary of state power nor a necessary accomplice to patriarchy[8] or capitalism (Donzelot, 1979, p. xx). The family does not take an homogeneous form, nor is it an indivisible unit. It is an 'uncertain form' divided by a complex grid of power relations some of which relate to age and sex and which may be a source of comfort in some contexts and horror in others. This makes *a priori* positions on the nature of the family reductionist and conceptually limiting. Rather, the family is a site of government whose destiny is linked in intricate ways to the destiny and social objectives of the nation. It is a socialising machine which plays a vital role in regulating individuals, curbing illegality and inculcating in children codes of personal conduct commensurate with the qualities of citizenship (Rose, 1989, pp. 126–30). The family is not a private sphere. On the contrary modern technologies of government have prised open the family, its conjugal relations and child rearing in particular, to new forms of visibility which are, in many respects, highly desirable in terms of mitigating patriarchal authority and other repressive forms of familial power.

The mechanisms which police the family are the same as those which give modern societies their particularly well-policed character (Donzelot, 1979, p. 7). These mechanisms are diffuse and multifarious. They do not emanate from any one source (i.e. the state) nor do they operate in terms of the logic of any single functionary of power, patriarchal or otherwise. They are not necessarily repressive and, for the most part, are productive and socially desirable. Modern technologies of government have sought, not to diminish the autonomy of the family, but to reorganise it in ways which strengthen and enhance the quality of the population. This is what Donzelot means by the 'policing of families.' He understands policing, as Foucault does also, not 'in the limiting repressive sense we give the term today', although it can be, but rather in a broader sense to mean the administration of family life through the institution and dispersion of new family forms, such as the child-centred nuclear family, and values (i.e. of hygiene and pedagogical norms) commensurate with social objectives, such as the enhanced prosperity of the social body. Families committed to the promotion of the physical and mental welfare of children 'have come to govern their intimate relations and socialise their children according to social norms but through the activation of their own hopes and fears' (Rose, 1989, p. 130) and generally not through mechanisms requiring direct coercion or force, such as the appropriation of children into State care. The adherence of families to social norms means two things. First, that the family has became the instrument, rather than the model, of government (Foucault, 1991, p. 100; Hirst, 1981, p. 74). Second, the fact that material and social benefit accrues to families which adhere to social norms provides the incentive for most to do so. This makes the families in these case studies exceptional examples of repressive governmental interventions into family life.

In the Australian context the government of the family has been achieved largely through mechanisms for the protection, education and health of children. Hence direct forms of State supervision over child rearing practices are unnecessary for the majority of Australian families. State supervision over families is rarely instituted and it would be a mistake to assume that families who fail to meet the standards expected of them by the authorities automatically come under departmental supervision. Many, precisely because of their marginality to urban centres, or their marginality to the gaze of governmental institutions such as baby health clinics or schools, may never come to the notice of the authorities. I am not suggesting that the gaze of the justice authorities is omnipotent—nor that all the diverse sites of governing families operate in tandem in a contrived fashion. The policing of families is much more accidental than this. However, this sample of families was not so random. All had come into the orbit of that gaze, albeit in a variety of ways—some through the school, others through the local baby health centre, some through the justice authorities and others through neighbours or relatives—and all were considered by the authorised family technicians to have failed in their civic duty as parents. Having been assessed as dysfunctional these families then came under a system of tutelage whereby their children were either supervised or removed and, in certain instances, were even incarcerated.

One may ask how this is possible given that within liberal democratic societies, such as Australia, intervention into family life exceeds the proper limits of the State and threatens the sacred autonomy of the family. Failure is what makes it possible. It is only through the failures of families that State and public powers find the means and the cause to legitimately intervene (Hirst, 1981, p. 73). Child abuse, juvenile delinquency, truancy and parental incompetence provide socially acceptable routes for State intervention, whereby children can be removed from families or placed under departmental supervision. So the autonomy of the family comes to depend not on legal rights, but on competence (Hirst, 1981, pp. 73–4). Families enjoy a loosely supervised freedom provided that they meet certain basic social expectations about sending their children to school, keeping them healthy and controlling their public conduct.

I am not suggesting that the government of the family is, in general terms, undesirable or essentially repressive. What I am suggesting here is that the social administration of family failure through disciplinary mechanisms such as juvenile justice and mandatory reporting schemes is largely ineffectual and often simply repressive. There is an urgent need for more innovative thinking about the social administration of family pathology. That thinking must focus on the means to provide the necessary incentives for families to become and remain committed to socially desirable objectives of good government such as the proper care and education of children. The provision of such incentives then rests heavily on the delivery of social and incomes policies of support for those sections of the community otherwise denied a means for sharing the prosperity of the nation and *not* on repressive child protection policies all too predictably directed at these same sections of the population. Where it is necessary for children to be removed from their families it is imperative that children taken into State care are provided with adequate social, emotional and income support and not lost in the system or locked up, as Christine and Kathy were.

The major problem I have with forms of government which operate through the family is not that they prise it open to new forms of social visibility, but that they lead to virtually no social provision being made for children not living in traditional family units. Family-less children are unsupported, exposed and vulnerable. Their marginality then pushes them into the hands of the welfare, along the fast track from care to detention and into the orbit of the criminal justice institutions. Just how this welfare/justice nexus operates is an issue of considerable importance which I return to in the concluding chapter.

6   Youth culture and female delinquency

Girls are less likely than boys to be channelled into the hands of the law enforcement authorities for their involvement in youth culture. The reason for this is simple. Fewer girls participate in the kinds of street-based youth culture (such as the graffiti gangs of the inner-city and Western suburbs) which bring so many boys into conflict with the law enforcement agencies. The spectacle of youth culture, while it is highly masculinised is, nevertheless, an important site from which *some* girls are channelled into the hands of the authorities. The reason for this is not so simple. The case notes of a girl who is referred to as Cheryl, provide the opportunity for exploring the reason why some girls are pushed into the hands of the authorities for participating in street-based youth culture. After summarising Cheryl's notes, this chapter offers several different (though not necessarily mutually exclusive) readings of her case.

Cheryl's case notes

When Cheryl was thirteen years old she appeared before the Children's Court for being uncontrollable. She had been absent from school for twenty-three days in term one and twenty-seven days in term two. It was not so much that she was absent from school but what she did during this absence that became the substance of the case against her. The court was informed of the following details of Cheryl's misconduct.

> Cheryl tends to associate with lesser desirable types in
> Campbelltown, particularly the Browns. Her brother, Roger, has not

set a very good example as he has been on probation and also an institutional inmate during his career as a juvenile. Cheryl first came to notice through the Campbelltown Public High School as she had been truanting in the company of (usually) Lisa Brown . . . Cheryl had also been involved in a couple of street fights with other girls outside the school premises. At an interview at the school Mrs Jones stated she could not control Cheryl. Prior to this I personally had seen Cheryl in the company of young men at the Hotel. Cheryl had admitted that she has visited hotels on other occasions. She is also permitted to go to discos and rock dances and usually does not arrive home until midnight. (Court Report, 5 August 1978)

Following the court appearance, Cheryl was released on probation under the following conditions: that she be of good behaviour, resume school forthwith and attend regularly, accept supervision, not associate with any person not approved by the district officer, continue to reside with her mother, and not be absent from home after 7.30 at night (Order of Children's Court, 5 August 1978). During the period of her probation Cheryl contested the authority of the district officer to supervise her 'freedom', choice of friends and leisure activities, ignoring instructions to dissociate with the Browns, her boyfriend and his group of friends. Her continued defiance resulted in court action for breaching the terms of her probation. The supervising district officer told the court that Cheryl did not like being told what to do, when to be home and with whom to socialise and concluded that:

At all times Cheryl has been extremely insolent and has not responded in any way to guidance or supervision from this department . . . At the time of the interview on 21/10/77 Cheryl stated that she would rather be locked up than have to make the effort to behave during the period of her probation. She seems to be of the opinion that a short committal is preferable to having people telling her what to do. She has no conception of right and wrong and is completely amoral. In view of Cheryl's defiance of any type of authority and lack of acceptance of any type of guidance it is felt that she would not respond effectively to a short period in training. *Recommendation*: Committal to a Training School for a Minimum of Six Months. (Court Report, 17 November 1978)

Cheryl appealed to the New South Wales District Court against the severity of her sentence, but lost. Once incarcerated, the fact that she could not apparently see anything wrong with her conduct or that of her peers continued to be documented in her case notes as a source of irritation to those delegated with the responsibility for her rehabilitation. The psychologist attached to the detention centre, for example, made the following assessment of her. In it he expressed considerable frustration with the difficulty he was encountering in working with Cheryl.

> Cheryl presented as an attractive girl, quietly confident of herself and her abilities. From what she says her mother appears to be quite ineffective in disciplining her and she is well aware that she can do as she pleases . . . She has no idea of what responsibility means in definition or in practice for any age group. She does believe that she has done no wrong in her opinion and says she doesn't budge from that opinion when she's right. It would help her to work with someone who has good rapport with her as to the basis of defining a right/wrong opinion. She tends to be self-centred and conscious of her appearance and herself on the whole. She finds school a bore as it seems she has little value for education, secondly she hopes to work in a milk bar for which it would seem education was fruitless. A milk bar to her signifies meeting a lot of people. To work with Cheryl in terms of counselling would be difficult as her mother she says has no objections and hence with this backing Cheryl has all the excuse she needs. (Psychological Assessment, 28/11/78)

After spending four months in a training school for truants, Cheryl was returned to her mother's care. Only three months passed, however, before the same district officer who had been previously delegated by the Children's Court to supervise Cheryl's freedom again took court action against her. And again the substance of the case against her, which appears below, focused almost entirely on Cheryl's involvement with other local youth in certain activities while truanting from school.

> Cheryl returned to school in February and was present until the 1/3/79 (a total of 6 days). She has been marked absent every day since. Attached is a copy of the medical certificate which covers Thursday and Friday for 'illness'. She was to resume school on the Monday and her mother believed that she had in fact gone back, but Cheryl wagged for the next week and a half. She was wagging school with Shelly who appeared before this court on Monday, for school default. While she was not at school she went to Georges milk bar, also Micks to play pool and Eddie's bar. Cheryl and another lass (aged 16) accompanied the lads who stole from the Hotel on Thursday (during school hours) and Cheryl is well aware of the poor reputations and previous court appearances for similar offences of most of the lads.
>
> Cheryl has yet again proved that she cannot keep to conditions placed on her by the Children's Court, and even the District Court. She has now obviously started to associate with those very much less desirable persons within the community as was previously anticipated prior to her original committal on 27/11/78.
>
> The lass is still only 13 years of age and still has at least two years of schooling to complete before she can leave school. She

states that she cannot cope with the work and does not like school for this reason. She is in fact a reasonably intelligent girl (I.Q. range 94–105 which is middle of the upper range) but her previous non-attendance would mean that she is not up to date with her lessons. Again there appears no alternative but to again recommend a committal for a minimum of six months. This will still provide Cheryl with the educational opportunities which she has missed out on over the past year or so and also it will allow her to grow a little older and gain more maturity and develop more self discipline so that further supervision later can provide her with the very best assistance possible . . . *Recommendation*: Committal to an institution for minimum period of six months. (Court Report, 14/3/79)

Throughout the many documents in Cheryl's criminal dossier, the same discourse recurs about the moral danger girls expose themselves to by participating in youth culture. Soon after Cheryl's release from custody, in a letter addressed to the superintendent, the supervising district officer went as far as to suggest that Cheryl's involvement in the local gang would inevitably lead to her falling pregnant:

Perusal of reports submitted during her detention clearly indicate that the girl's mother cannot effectively supervise her; that she spends her time with young undesirable adults much older than herself; that she frequents hotels and that she has already been involved in sexual activity. In the short time she has been home she has gravitated to her former pattern of living. It will not be long before she will be an applicant for Family Assistance. (Letter to Superintendent, 13 December 1979).

Two more examples from psychological assessments in Cheryl's case notes should suffice to illustrate the point.

She (Cheryl) has good recreational skills like squash, tennis, cricket, football, swimming. But seems to spend more leisure time walking the streets, 'chucking laps' i.e. racing up and down in cars, (and) motor bike riding; the latter are types of recreation that seem to draw attention to herself and hence tends to indulge in them more. (Psychological Assessment, 28 November 1978)
She has a mixed group of peers from school kids up to adults (21-22) who like hanging around shopping centres and going to home parties. She stays away from home at night. Therefore Cheryl has developed a pattern of having her own way, she is quite egocentric in many respects and fails to see why others should determine what she should do. (Psychological Assessment, 30 March 1979)

There are several ways of reading the interaction between Cheryl and the justice authorities described in the notes above. One way of taking up the issue is to argue that Cheryl's involvement with the 'local gang' was a form of resistance to the imposition of compulsory schooling and her policing was a form of social control; an explicit attempt to contain the threat of working-class youth culture to the hegemony of conventional middle-class culture. The first reading makes the case for such an analysis. Alternatively Cheryl's participation in street culture can be read as a defiance of the boundaries of a culture of femininity, which define the bedroom as the proper place for adolescent female culture. Her criminalisation can then be seen as a punishment for transgressing the limits of those boundaries. The second reading makes the case for such an analysis. Another, but by no means definitive, reading of Cheryl's notes analyses the policing of her participation in youth culture as an exercise in the government of youth.

Youth culture and delinquency: a cultural studies analysis

Since the mid-1970s it has been commonplace to analyse the emergence of youth culture and its policing in terms of the theoretical model developed by a team of researchers attached to the Centre for Contemporary Cultural Studies (CCCS) at Birmingham University (Tait, 1992, p. 12). In that model, youth subcultures are defined as a subset of larger cultural configurations—which in modern societies are considered to be class cultures (Clarke *et al.* in Hall and Jefferson, 1975, p. 13). For working-class children this culture is that of their parents.

According to this analytical model, youth subcultures form in the space between parent culture and dominant culture, expressing the generational specificity of lived class experience. In other words, youth subcultures seek to 'win space' between parent culture and dominant culture, albeit, only symbolic. The model then turns to the concept of generational consciousness to explain the relationship of double articulation between youth subcultures and parent cultures. While it is acknowledged that youth subcultures differentiate themselves from parent culture through distinct focal concerns, style and activities it is argued that youth subcultures also share with their parents a working-class culture subordinate in relation to the dominant bourgeois culture (Clarke *et al.* in Hall and Jefferson, 1975, p. 13). This is why the spectacular youth subcultures of the post-war era are recognised in this model as part of the continuum of working-class culture.

One of the arguments central to this model is that the emergence of spectacular post-war youth subcultures (such as the teddy boys, mods, rockers and skinheads in Britain, and bikies, sharpies, bodgies and widgies in Australia), arose out of more fundamental changes in the class structure of post-war class societies. The argument goes something like this. Changes in the local economy disturbed a particular working-class culture, dismantled particular balances and stabilities and reshaped historical givens around which working-class culture had previously developed. This resulted in changes in housing, kinship patterns and in the ecology of the working-class neighbourhood (Clarke *et al.* in Hall and Jefferson, 1975, p. 36). The CCCS theorists identified five historical changes to post-war British society which they say provided the impetus for the emergence of post-war youth subcultures.[1] In Australia, Stratten has identified a number of similar historical changes which he says made possible the emergence of the consumption-based youth cultures of the 1950s and 1960s, such as the bodgies and widgies (Stratten, 1992, pp. 2–12).

Within this theoretical framework acts of juvenile delinquency which arise in the context of the spectacle of youth culture (that is, doin' nothin', havin' a laugh', smashin' a few bottles commonplace among urban working-class kids' street culture; the 'poofter bashing' and 'paki bashing' of the teddy boys; the intra-violence of football hooliganism; and the bashings of migrants by bodgies in the 1950s) come to be celebrated as oppositional elements of working-class youth culture, as 'resistance through rituals', while attempts to police it are frequently denounced as coercive state interventions, or forms of social control. The street is identified in this body of work as the traditional site of working-class youth culture. This is apparently why the street has become a site of contestation between the authentic bearers of working-class culture and the agencies of repressive state apparatuses who are sent in to police the use of public space. Within the discursive terms of this model, to participate in youth subculture is then to participate in class struggle. Youth culture becomes not only a site of leisure and conspicuous consumption, but also a site of disorder and struggle 'with the forces of middle-class morality' (Stratten, 1992, p. 21), albeit only symbolically.

Many of the studies of youth culture using this model have been British. There has, however, been some research on Australian youth cultures which uses this model of analysis. Notable examples are Stratten's analysis of the emergence of bodgies and widgies in Australia in the 1950s (Stratten, 1992) and another is the research on bikies by Cunneen, Lynch, Tupper and Findlay (Cunneen *et al.*, 1989). Both of these pieces of research provide detailed historical explanations of the emergence of youth cultures in Australia, following the formulae of the CCCS model fairly closely. In the tradition of the CCCS model Stratten, for example, attributes the emergence of bodgies and widgies as Australia's first post-war working-class youth culture to a number of historical changes to the Australian economy and society. Among these, Stratten's careful research identifies an explosion of interest in American youth culture due to the presence of American troops in Australia during the late 1940s; the ideological acceptance of the teenager as a cultural category; the changing consumption patterns and increasing visibility of working-class youth culture (during a period of growing full employment in the post-war economy); and the proliferation of consumer products aimed at the youth market such as records, films, magazines, clothes and cars under conditions of economic liberality during Australia's period of post-war industrialisation (Stratten, 1992, pp. 2–10). Stratten argues that the public image of the bodgie style defined it as a deviant youth culture posing a threat to the moral and social fabric of Australian society (Stratten, 1992, p. 88). This folk devil image then led to the classification of the working-class youth who participated in the production and consumption of the bodgie style as delinquent, rather than, Stratten argues, as just ordinary young people enjoying the new consumption patterns and visibility of working-class culture (Stratten, 1992, p. 190). Stratten concludes that:

> The effect was to give a new visibility to many working-class youth activities which, taken out of context and combined with the confusion over the teenager, became the source of a moral panic in which the lead characters, the mythical bodgie and widgie, became folk devils of truly demonic proportions who seemed to strike at the very basis of the (middle class) social and moral order. (Stratten, 1992, pp. 196–7)

The theoretical framework of the CCCS model of youth subcultures and neo-Marxist variations of it have been used in research as the key to unlock the reason why so much policing has as its focus working-class youth and their participation in the spectacle of youth culture (see, for example, Cunneen, 1985; Hall et al., 1978; Hebdige, 1978; Humphries, 1981; Pearson, 1983; White, 1990). As a way of demonstrating the utility of the CCCS model, I shall now use it to produce a reading of Cheryl's notes.

Some of what this theoretical model says about the policing of youth culture finds a good deal of empirical confirmation in a certain reading of Cheryl's case. For example, the social ecology of the working-class neighbourhood in which she lived had undergone massive social and economic disruption in the post-war period. An influx of immigrants and public housing projects converged upon Campbelltown during the 1970s. The area underwent a rapid urbanisation process leading to significant shifts in the local economy and its class structure; one of which was a massive increase in the youth population which doubled in the five-year period during which Cheryl was growing up.[2] Campbelltown also had one of the highest rates of detection for female delinquency in the State (Carrington, 1989, p. 467). Cheryl lived in a housing commission dwelling with an older brother, who had previously appeared before the Children's Court, and a mother who worked as a domestic at the local hospital and who earned less than the average wage. She obviously came from a working-class family background. The changes in the class structure and social ecology of her neighbourhood, it could be said, provided the impetus for the emergence of a counter-school culture as well as a street culture among the working-class youth of Campbelltown in which Cheryl participated, spending most of her leisure time riding up and down the streets on the back of a motorbike.

Cheryl's truancy and involvement in the 'local gang' is then open to the suggestion that it was a form of resistance to the assaults on the organic culture of Campbelltown's working-class youth. By continuing to defy the instructions issued by the supervising officer it could also be said that Cheryl was asserting the legitimacy of her involvement in that culture. A whole body of literature associates street culture with working-class youth (Hall and Jefferson, 1975; Corrigan, 1979, p. 119; Blanch in Clarke, Cricher and Johnson, 1979, p. 103; Robins and Cohen, 1978; White, 1990). In certain restricted respects her participation in the 'local gang' can therefore be conceived as an expression of generational autonomy from her parent working-class culture which nevertheless maintained some fundamental identifications with it—such as the focus on the street and activities associated with working-class youth.

The behaviour of Cheryl's mother, by seeking to protect her daughter from the intrusions of 'the welfare', is also open to the suggestion that she was resisting the imposition of a middle-class culture. She was represented in the official documents put before the Children's Court as the kind of mother who allowed her children too much freedom, who let them run wild on the streets and who encouraged her daughter's delinquencies. Delinquency is located in this discourse as having a clear association with the culture of working-class parents and that of their mothers in particular.

While the cultural studies model has much to commend it, it has at least three major problems as a way of explaining the policing of youth culture and Cheryl's participation in it. First, the 'discovery' of youth subcultures in the mid-nineteenth century undercuts the theoretical proposition developed by the cultural studies model that spectacular youth subcultures are a distinctively post-war phenomenon. Youth subcultures can be traced to the emergence of a sociological gaze in the 1830s and 1840s which sought to identify, classify and make subcultures socially visible (Tolsen, 1990, pp. 113–25). During this period the emergence of charitable bodies and the mobilisation of public opinion about the 'wandering tribes' and young 'costermongers' of London gave rise to a number of discourses about youth culture and a series of legislative and social reforms aimed at saving children from it (Hebdige, 1988, pp. 20–1). Thus, as Tolsen argues:

> In the post-war period, youth subcultures may have re-emerged in their characteristic modern forms; but the conditions and criteria for their recognition seem to have a much more extended history.
> (Tolsen, 1990, p. 114)

A second difficulty I have with the cultural studies model concerns its assumption that those agencies who police youth are acting in the interests of the capitalist state with one purpose—to control young people; what Connell has called, 'the contraceptive theory of youth culture' (Connell, 1983, p. 230). Charitable bodies, educational institutions, both private and public, church groups, neighbourhood centres, kinship structures, families, welfare agencies, youth refuges and other such agencies operate outside and sometimes alongside state agencies in their efforts to normalise the conduct of delinquent or troublesome youth. Cheryl's mother, for example, at the same time as making efforts to protect Cheryl from 'the welfare', pursued her own independent efforts to normalise her daughter's delinquencies. By locating the source, means and motivation for the correction of delinquency and the policing of Cheryl's involvement in the local youth culture in the capitalist state and its law enforcement agencies, many of the other, and perhaps more significant, sites which seek to regulate youth are overlooked. The family, for example, can hardly be overlooked as one of the key sites for the policing of girls' participation in the spectacle of youth culture. The suggestion that youth subcultures are an effect of the post-war restructuring of class relations, and that their policing is a form of social control designed to manage the threat they pose to the dominant cultural order, lacks plausibility when we come to analyse specific instances where such policing is said to have occurred. Perhaps this is more the case for girls than it is with boys.

A further difficulty I have with the model is that the discursive formation of the category of juvenile delinquency has shifted and multiplied in the present such that it can no longer be said that delinquency is directly associated with working-class youth culture by the governmental apparatuses that police it. Discourses about delinquency have shifted from the nineteenth century discourses of eugenics and Lombrosian criminology which did identify a whole class or race of children as delinquent (that is larrikins); to child-saving discourses which located poverty and deprivation as the primary cause of juvenile delinquency; to twentieth century psychological discourses which have sought to classify and measure delinquency as the product of a range of *individual* and familial deficits in association with contemporary social work discourses which see delinquency as the product of malfunctioning families and pathological communities.[3] In these latter discursive frameworks adolescence as a *period* of rebellion has replaced the cultural category of *youth* as having a perceived relation with delinquency, rather than the other way round as suggested in the CCCS model. Youth-as-delinquent is now predominantly understood as a stage and not a station in life,[4] and as an individual failure rather than a collective responsibility. This is what I have referred to as deficit discourses throughout this book and consider in specific detail in a later chapter. The point is, official discourse, by recognising that children can and do grow out of crime, provided that they are managed in a certain way so as to prevent the development of a delinquent career, are operating on the assumption that delinquency is a stage and not a station in life (Standing Committee on Social Issues, Juvenile Justice, 1992; Annual Report, YACS, 1990). This discursive shift is important because it has led to the proliferation of individualised forms of therapeutic intervention (that is, psychological) for dealing with the 'problem child'. These forms of intervention are considered more fully in a subsequent reading of Cheryl's notes.

A final point I raise as a major limitation of the cultural studies model for analysing the policing of girls participation in youth culture is one which many feminists have already stressed. Given the almost wholesale neglect of gender in this model it has limited usefulness in explaining the policing of girls participation in youth culture and the acts of delinquency alleged to arise from that participation. While the street is a significant, if not the most significant, site for channelling boys into the hands of the justice authorities, this is *not* necessarily the case with girls for whom schools and families are probably just as, if not more, significant in this process.

The culture of femininity and female delinquency

The romanticisation of youth subculture has met with considerable criticism for its emphasis on age and class and its almost wholesale neglect of race, ethnicity and gender. A compelling body of feminist critique has taken issue with both the content of youth subcultures, their theorisation within cultural studies and their usefulness in

explaining girls' participation in either delinquency or youth subcultures. The feminist critique has taken issue with the sexist
elements of counter-school cultures, punk, skinhead, teddy boy and
other youth subcultures and the fact that they have passed largely
unnoticed by those celebrating them as the bastions of working-class
rebellion. Feminists claim that while girls may have played only a
minor role in the emergence of spectacular post-war youth subcultures this nevertheless does not excuse male researchers of youth
subcultures for completely ignoring the significance of gender. They
argue that the marginalisation of girls in these male-dominated
subcultures is symptomatic of the broader subordination of women
in patriarchal societies. McRobbie (1991) suggests that whatever
working-class youth subcultures resolve or resist about dominant
culture, they cannot be regarded as examples of progressive masculinity. She points out that girls who participate in male-dominated
youth subcultures often do so on unequal terms. Their membership
in a subculture is usually through an attachment to a boyfriend and
girls are often excluded from the central subcultural activities of the
particular group. While this reinforces unequal sexual relations
because it produces a dependence of girls on boys for access to and
participation in cultural activities (McRobbie and Garber in Hall
and Jefferson, 1975), it also reduces the likelihood of girls getting
into trouble with the law by being involved in the activities of youth
culture. Indeed, a major reason for their much lower rates of
detection for juvenile offending is precisely because so few girls
participate in street-based spectacular youth subcultures.

Out of that critique and on the assumption that girls are either
absent from, or marginal to, most working-class youth subcultures,
feminist researchers have developed a concept of a culture of
femininity to explain the leisure forms of girls. That girls negotiate
a different social space to boys is absolutely central to the concept
of a culture of femininity. Boys are thought to occupy the public
world for their leisure and subcultural activities, while girls are
thought to resort to the private sanctuary of the bedroom, where
they read teeny-bopper magazines and indulge in fantasies with their
girlfriends about rock stars and *Dolly* pin-ups (McRobbie, 1991).
The marginality of girls from street culture is seen as a product of
the subordination of women more generally. Girls who enter the
male territory of the street, or the subculture, are said to do so on
male terms, as girlfriends, appendages, whores, sluts, moles and
prostitutes (Lees, 1986).

The notion of a culture of femininity is, in certain respects, useful
in understanding why Cheryl was punished by the courts for *not*
participating in that culture. Cheryl's leisure activities clearly did
not fit the prescription of a culture of femininity. She routinely

invaded the male space of the street and the local youth subculture, spending her leisure time 'walking the streets, "chucking laps" i.e. racing up and down in cars, and motor bike riding' (Psychological Assessment, 28 November 1979). She did not confine her cultural activities to the bedroom, or at least not her own. Efforts to remove her from the street through intensive supervision and the imposition of curfew limitations can therefore be seen as attempts to force Cheryl to live within the boundaries of a culture of femininity. When this failed Cheryl was punished with court action resulting in her committal to a detention centre. Cheryl was being punished by the courts for her invasion into the male territory of street-based youth culture. It could then be suggested that the juvenile justice system operates on a double standard of morality, punishing girls and not boys for their participation in the spectacle of youth culture.

The difficulty with this argument, of course, is that it reduces the operation of juvenile justice to a single unitary discourse about sexuality. While I do not intend to repeat the critique of this form of feminist analysis from Chapter 1, a few specific problems with it need addressing here as they also resonate within feminist cultural studies. The first major difficulty with this argument is that, in numerical terms many more boys than girls are criminalised for their participation in youth culture. In Australia, this is particularly so with Aboriginal boys involved in 'joy-riding', car theft, or just hanging around the streets. So it is rather odd to argue that there is a double standard which punishes *only* girls for their participation in street culture. Perhaps girls are chastised for different kinds of public conduct than boys, and discourses of sexuality certainly enter into the policing of girls who fail to govern their bodies in public so as not to arouse male desire (see Judy's case notes in Chapter 1). However, to *ignore* the fact that it is more frequently boys who are criminalised for their involvement in visible forms of youth culture is a curious omission indeed. Then to suggest that the street is unequivocally male territory glosses over significant forms of contestation between groups of men (that is male police officers and Aboriginal boys; railway patrol guards and graffiti 'bombers') over that territory and its consequences for particular cultural categories of men (that is the high rates of criminalisation among Aboriginal boys and boys from the Western suburbs of Sydney).

The second major difficulty I have with the concept of a culture of femininity is that, by positioning girls as passive victims of the male gaze, the possibility is overlooked that girls such as Cheryl may actually negotiate street culture as a site of pleasure and not exploitation. The culture of femininity, as conceived within this discourse, does not allow for the possibility that girls actively seek and exploit opportunities for excitement or pleasure. That culture is pre-packed, sanitised, sold and consumed by the docile unimaginative girl. When girls do enter the 'male' territory of the street or the subculture it is only through the 'male gaze'. Unlike the objects of style of male youth subcultures, the objects of style in the culture of femininity (for example, magazines such as *Jackie* and *Dolly* and rock idols such as Michael Jackson) are unnegotiable. This reading of the culture of femininity patronises girls as the passive consumers of romantic individualism—and not the exciting authors of girls' cultures centred around focal concerns and social spaces in vital respects different to boys. Just because many of these cultural activities are less visible does not necessarily mean that they are more or less exciting, more or less oppressive and so on.

Certainly, Cheryl was neither a passive victim of the culture of femininity nor of the juvenile justice system. She actively sought excitement through her participation in youth culture, 'chucking laps', and riding up and down on motor bikes, and was prepared to risk breaking the terms of her probation to continue to do so. When confronted with attempts to thwart her involvement in the local youth culture she went down kicking every time, resisting attempts to remove her from the street, put back in her bedroom, isolated from her peers and separated from her boyfriend. It cost her two short committals to a juvenile detention centre but, as Cheryl once stated in an interview with her supervising district officer:

> . . . she would rather be locked up than have to make the effort to behave during her period of probation. She seems to be of the opinion that a short committal is preferable to having people telling her what to do (Court Report, 17 November 1978).

The government of youth culture and delinquency

Childhood has become one of the most intensely governed sectors of personal life (Rose, 1989, p. 188). Because youth is a passage into citizenship through which all adults of the social body must invariably pass its management is considered absolutely crucial to the good government of the population. Delinquency is just one of many deviations requiring management along the path from childhood to successful citizenship. Most of these deviations are normalised in their sites of authorship without recourse to more coercive intervention from the justice authorities.

As the CCCS model points out, youth subcultures form in the space between the multiple disciplines of the family, the school and the workplace (Hebdige, 1988, p. 35). They thus compete with these sites in the governmentalisation of youth and this is why youth culture poses a particular problem for the government of childhood.

I am not suggesting that they defy governance. On the contrary, they could be said to entail forms of governance which operate through the medium of youth culture and teenage consumerism. The point is that youth cultures tend to defy, test and rebel against existing forms of governmentality which operate through the school, the family, the workplace and organised leisure. They are then able to create a heterotopia, 'a sort of simultaneously mythic and real contestation of the space in which we live' (Foucault, 1986, p. 24),[3] by disrupting the normative symbols and utensils of conventional cultures. In the chemistry of opposing cultural forms an explosive juncture occurs,[4] creating the possibility for disrupting conventional norms about sex, class, race, adolescence, fashion, style, time, space and so on. The heterotopia of youth culture provides a space within which boys *and* girls can experiment with their sexual identity, deconstruct the boundaries of gender, refuse the naturalness of heterosexuality and disrupt the sexualised images of the body. The style of 'mod' for example, creates for the girls who participate in it a suspended sexuality—a time for negotiating sex, exploring style and playing with language in a space which evades parental surveillance and disrupts the male gaze. Like Madonna, girls can use the products of youth culture to reinvent themselves 'in ways that challenge the stable notion of gender as the edifice of sexual difference' (Schwichtenberg, 1993, p. 132).

Cheryl's involvement in the local gang is not just a means of expressing generational autonomy from the culture of her parents while at the same time remaining within its orbit of safety. Neither is her involvement in the local youth culture simply a means of testing the boundaries of a culture of femininity. She and her friends were creating a heterotopia of delinquency, a time and place which disrupted norms about sexuality, femininity, leisure, social status and adolescence; a heterotopia at once interior and exterior to Cheryl's lived experience of class and sex. The space was the street (where girls are not meant to be); the time was after dark (when girls are meant to be home) or between the hours of 9.00 a.m. and 3.00 p.m. (when young people are supposed to be at school); the cultural object was the car or the motor bike (which girls in their femininity are not meant to desire); the associations were undesirable youth (with whom chaste girls do not associate); and the technology of government was youth culture.

Cheryl is not atypical of the youths who are routinely processed through the juvenile justice system. She came from a poor socio-economic background; lived in a housing commission dwelling; had a sibling who had been before the Children's Court; had herself rebelled against the requirements of the school system at an early age; participated in a youth culture centred on visible street activities which defied the dominant norms of family life and schooling; and, when confronted with attempts to correct her ways by welfare officials and the courts, she rejected these as well. The basis of her incarceration is quite transparent: not the commission of any legal offence, but the repeated and escalating transgression of 'infra-legal' norms governing adolescence and family life.

More than half of the girls who pass through the Children's Court are charged with criminal offences, although it would be wrong to assume that the means by which they are criminalised differ in any vital respect from Cheryl's experience. The commission of a discrete offence is of restricted relevance in the process, as the substantial non-criminalisation of youthful offending indicates. Most offending is relatively petty, attracts no official notice and is reconcilable with and through the normalisation of its authors in family, school and organised leisure. Youths like Cheryl tend to pass into the hands of district officers, police, the courts, juvenile incarceration and their auxiliary forms of expertise (psychologists and social workers) only if and when their offences and/or other forms of 'misconduct' breach these normalising standards and expectations. Cheryl's behaviour appears to do this at every step along the path to her incarceration.

Along the path of her governmentalisation through juvenile justice Cheryl was classified and measured according to pedagogic standards and psychological discourses.[5] She was supervised and assessed according to the logics of social work[6] and punished according to the advice of the experts.[7] She was sent to an institution, that great asylum of the modern epoch, and subject to a range of carceral disciplines. Normalisation through incarceration failed, as it often does.[8] The process repeated itself. Cheryl was supervised, assessed, classified and punished by the invocation of a range of discourses. She contested attempts to govern her leisure through the mechanism of departmental supervision.[9] She was again sent to an institution according to the logics of social work and the advice of the experts.[10]

An intelligible logic of social control appears to be at work in the process of policing Cheryl's participation in youth culture. Those who cannot or refuse to be governed in the relatively private sites of the family, the school and organised leisure are, regardless of their crimes, vulnerable to being handed over to the agents of carceral discipline and criminalisation. Their marginality (and that of their family and peers) to the other sites of government places them within the orbit of criminalising practices and institutions.

There are two ways of interpreting and taking up this critical point. The first would see it as being an extension of the argument contained in the structuralist readings offered above: that is, as a form of class or patriarchal control within which ideological and cultural apparatuses operate alongside repressive apparatuses of control—consensual participation in the former always in some sense operating in the shadow of penality. Schooling, welfare, family, organised leisure and other 'private' measures of government would therefore be seen as extensions of state control; as embodying the same concerns, norms, practices as overt agencies of control, but perhaps more pervasively and insidiously for being the more discreet and privatised.

The major problem with this argument, however, is its inherent implausibility. The eighteenth and nineteenth century reformers who sought such extended tutelary measures over the young and their families were not mere agents of the state and their initiatives and demands were not of a unitary nature. Many of the demands and practices of government of the young in the nineteenth century emanated from heterogeneous sources *outside* the liberal state, and *against* what was perceived to be the juridical straitjacket in which it operated—entailing therefore 'not so much the estatisation of society, as the "governmentalisation" of the state' (Foucault, 1991, p. 103). Social interventions, such as compulsory education, child-saving philanthropy, child welfare practice and juvenile justice, emerged as strategies for governing children, alongside other modern forms of governmentality for managing the social body. The governmental apparatuses for correcting and managing youth operate through a variety of mechanisms and institutions, some of which can be located in the social administration of the state,[11] but many of which cannot. Schooling, for example, comes to incorporate a range of regimes of training and discipline—intellectual, moral, physical and social—and is directed at the young (Hunter, 1988; Chapter 3). As I said earlier in Chapter 3, there is obviously room for debate about the nature and effects of schooling practice in the past and present, but only the very crudest social control theory would seek to abstract out of such diversity a unitary imperative of control. Clearly, a multiplicity of discourses, norms and practices were invoked in the governmentalisation of Cheryl's conduct. Likewise, such diversity cannot usefully be reduced to a single logic of control or form of sovereign power, be it class, patriarchal or otherwise.

A second way of taking up the point is to recognise the specificity of these sites of government *and* also their interconnectedness. Schools, families and other agencies routinely avoid resorting to the agencies of juvenile justice in circumstances where this is an option. Daily events in families, playgrounds, sports stadiums and school rooms could be treated as police matters if teachers, parents, neighbours and administrators were minded to do so. They refrain, presumably because they implicitly subordinate a concern with formal legal rationality to the rationalities of governance which operate within the school, community and family environments—the substantive objectives to care, educate and train the young to which these sites and institutions are committed. They also have available to them their own sanctions and modes of discipline. This is particularly so in private schools where parents enter into a contractual arrangement allowing the school authorities to institute privatised forms of governance over their children. It is not necessary to depict these as entirely benign, constructive or effective institutions. The point is rather that they are not the necessary effect of the essential structure of society (capitalist, patriarchal) and the replication of its logic of control throughout the institutions of social government. On the contrary, they entail limited and particular norms, knowledges and techniques of governance. The efficacy of these can be debated, but only usefully in their detail and particularity and relative to the *positive* as well as the negative capacities (intellectual aptitudes, technical skills such as reading and writing, civic responsibilities) they aspire to confer on the young.

Rather than seeing in families, schools, child welfare institutions and other apparatuses of government a hidden extension of social control, perhaps more attention should be given to the specific objectives and practices of social administration as they relate to the positive processes of the formation of citizenry through the government of youth. From the particular perspective of this chapter's concern with the interrelationship of these sites of government and the juvenile justice system, a major issue arises as to how these other institutions (especially schools and families) could more adequately serve to insulate girls such as Cheryl from the carceral discipline of judicial forms of government.

The so-called 'failures', such as Cheryl, are frequently subjected to measures of government that are both repressive and futile. Far from having some obvious (if latent) functionality, they manifest the limitations of policing children through forms of government which rely on child welfare measures and juvenile justice provisions. It would be a mistake to see the subjection of youth to various forms and practices of government as a denial of some authentic, pre-governed state of freedom or to posit some 'ideal of complete personal development' realisable only in the 'complete development' of civilisation and culture (that is, socialism) (Hunter, 1988, pp. 113–21). The category and meanings of youth are themselves the *products* of specific governing practices and cultural technologies—of a certain organisation of familial practices and of pedagogic regimes of various kinds. To note their historical and cultural variability is not to deny the necessity of forms of

government of the young or to assume that they can be written out
of social relations or, in many instances, even easily changed.
As has already been noted, many of these governmental
mechanisms confer positive capabilities, such as literacy and
citizenship on the young, as well as protecting them against
exploitation and oppression of various kinds (for example the early
factory Acts which removed from children the 'freedom' to sell their
labour in mines and factories; and the age of consent legislation
discussed in Chapter 1). Such complexity cannot usefully be reduced
to a simple problematic of social control, to negation or repression,
capitalist, patriarchal or otherwise. Nevertheless, there is a sense in
which it could be said that the moral panic over youth is a perennial
if not permanent feature of the modern social body. Youth has
become a metaphor for trouble, uncertainty, hooliganism and
delinquency. Youth, as students, delinquents or gang members, have
been constituted and reconstituted as folk devils, as 'visible
reminders of what we should not be' (Cohen, 1980, p. 10). But I
am not disputing that youth are intensely governed or policed. What
I am suggesting is that the preoccupation with the government of
the young is not simply an effect of moral panic, or an artifice of
popular ignorance, fear or media beat-ups. Families, parents, youths,
teachers, youth workers, police, even the authors and readers of
articles on youth cultures, are inescapably involved in daily
reflection and practice concerning these issues of government in
their own lives and in relation to others. Attempts to isolate and
localise such questions in the state or a unified conception of social
control, tend (where they are more than merely gestural in nature)
to suggest that these are matters that are capable of revolutionary
transcendence. This is a flight from reality which seriously detracts
from the necessary tasks of reflection and invention in and on the
present.

   Cheryl's case is open to multiple readings. While I have only
presented three I am not suggesting that they exhaust all such
possibilities, nor that the readings are mutually exclusive. Clearly,
Cheryl's notes can be read in a way which emphasises the role and
importance of law enforcement agencies in the social control of
young people—as exemplary of the multiplication of the sites and
mechanisms for policing youth culture and punishing girls who flout
the bounds of the culture of femininity by participating in them.
The first and second readings contained elements of this kind of
analysis. The third reading displaces the totalising, negativistic
concept of social control with the concept of governmentality. The
governmentalisation of youth should not be interpreted in a simple
negative sense, as the policing of youth in ways commensurate with
a particular social order. Starting from the premise that it is not

only utopian, but highly undesirable, to imagine a world without the government of conduct, the debate is not about the necessity of policing *per se*, but the desirability of different technologies of government over others and their particular consequences for specific categories of youth, such as girls like Cheryl.

7   Sex, youth and justice: 'In her best interests'

Earlier chapters have examined the school, the leisure venue and the family as the principal sites where the government of children and youth occur and from where girls such as Cheryl and Terese were channelled into the orbit of the juvenile justice agencies. However, the management of delinquency, of all of those minor but regular transgressions of the infra-legal norms of adolescence, rarely occurs through juvenile justice intervention. Most is dealt with at the site of authorship—family, school or at play—with few repercussions for the author. Parents, teachers and others responsible for the government of youth have their own particular modes of discipline and thus routinely avoid recourse to the law in dealing with delinquency. In the majority of cases, then, which end up before the Children's Court the conduct regarded as aberrant is in vital respects no different from that dealt with on a daily basis by agencies outside the legal system. The only difference is that juvenile justice is the mechanism through which these delinquencies are managed, rather than the family, the school or some other intermediary. The governmentalisation of these young people is taken over by a network of State agencies allegedly concerned with their welfare. They then become subsumed into the discourses about 'problem youth' and are managed through a variety of disciplinary techniques which generally do not distinguish the abused child from the 'delinquent'.

We know from self-report studies that delinquency is a type of behaviour which is widely dispersed throughout the adolescent population. It is reasonable to ask, therefore, why so relatively few

girls are recruited into the official population of delinquents from
this very large cohort of potential recruits? What makes some girls
so much more vulnerable to official detection than others for the
commission of minor typically adolescent, misdemeanours—
truanting, parental defiance, shop-lifting, sexual promiscuity, fare
evasion or offensive behaviour. This vulnerability is certainly not
random given the concentration of the detection rates for female
delinquency in the most marginalised sectors of the community, in
housing commission areas and Aboriginal communities in particular.
What interests me is precisely how the juvenile justice agencies
manage to gain access to specific girls by penetrating the sites which
ordinarily govern youth, normalise their delinquencies, and insulate
them from criminalisation. With a view to answering some of these
questions this chapter provides an account of the mechanics of the
criminalisation process through which both the girls in this study
and their families were processed.

Dissolving the welfare/justice dichotomy

The separation of Children's Courts from adult courts has been
commonly identified as the point at which a welfare model was
grafted onto the administration of juvenile justice. In New South
Wales this occurred in 1905 when the *Neglected Children and
Juvenile Offenders Act*, which provided for the establishment of a
separate jurisdiction for children, was enacted. The Children's Court
was supposed to dissolve the juridical nature of court proceedings,
rid the court of the rhetorical jousting between the defence and the
crown, and dispose of cases according to a broader logic recognising
the special status and needs of children by taking into consideration
the welfare of the child, his/her family background and other individual circumstances. Significantly, the Children's Court had the
jurisdiction to hear matters relating not only to juvenile offending,
but also to child welfare, as in cases of parental incompetence and
neglect. This meant that children as victims and offenders appeared
before the same courts and became largely undifferentiated in
Children's Court proceedings.

The emphasis on informalism, rehabilitation, custodial
alternatives and on elevating the needs and not the deeds of the
child, have been widely conceived as the virtues of a welfare model
of justice. The justice model has been counterposed as overly
punitive, legalistic, juridical and mystifying to those brought before
it. The reality is that juvenile justice administration has fallen far
short of fulfilling anything like these two counter-posed idealised
visions of justice. This has then led many commentators from a

Minda Children's Court, *1965. (Reproduced with kind permission of N.S.W. Department of Community Services.)*

variety of perspectives to attribute the problems in the administration of juvenile justice, such as the lumping together of neglected and delinquent children, and the abuses of children's rights in the system, to the competing demands between legalism on one hand and welfarism on the other (Harris and Webb, 1987, p. 12). Consequently, much of the debate about reform has centred around the effects of grafting welfare provisions into the juvenile justice arena (Anderson, 1978; Goldstein *et al.*, 1980; Morris *et al.*, 1980). According to the terms of this debate the welfare approach has, on the one hand, displaced the hard hand of the law with the gentle touch of rehabilitation while, on the other, it has displaced due process with a blatant disregard for the rights of children and their families.

I would suggest, however, that the shifts in punishment which take the welfare of the child as a guiding principle in the administration of penality have a much longer and more complicated genealogy than one which sees them simply beginning with the separation of adult and children jurisdictions. The reduction of penal severity in the administration of criminal justice over the last two hundred years has been at the cost of the proliferation of more generalised and less visible forms of punishment often carried out not by the court, but by a host of pathologists and functionaries that surround it (Foucault, 1977). This has occurred in both adult and juvenile jurisdictions and has had curiously demonstrative effects on the processing of child welfare cases. These effects are considered in more detail in the latter half of this chapter.

The point relevant to my argument here is that the conception of juvenile justice as a system of counterposing tensions between two apparently opposing models, of punishment (judicial) on the one hand, and welfare (non-judicial) on the other, overlooks the strategic alliance that has emerged between welfare and justice and its effects on child welfare (Burchell, 1979, pp. 242–4). In the pages which follow I argue that one of the major effects of this strategic alliance has been the marginalisation of judicial logic and the concomitant de-centring of the Children's Court. Another has been a strong and enduring nexus between justice and welfare resulting in the punishment of girls like Judy, who end up as welfare cases before the courts. The following deals with each of these issues in turn.

The dispersion of judicial power

The Children's Courts in New South Wales deal mostly with cases of 'admitted' or 'negotiated' guilt which are estimated to comprise about 95 per cent of all cases (Youth Justice Coalition, 1990). As a result of this the primary function of the court is to determine outcomes and administer punishment and not to determine guilt or test evidence. Those in a position to determine outcomes are not magistrates, but a range of social work, educative and psychological agents who supply the court with the necessary information upon which such decisions are ordinarily based. In fact the Children's Court is required to do this. The *Child Welfare Act* 1939 (NSW), under Section 89/2, instructs magistrates in making an order (sentencing) to give consideration to reports 'setting out the details and results of investigation into antecedents, home environment, companions, education, school attendance, habits, recreation, characters, reputation, disposition, medical history and physical or mental characteristics or defects, if any, of the child or young person'. The legislation which has replaced the *Child Welfare Act* 1939 (NSW) allows for similar provisions[1] in the disposition of cases. Thus the Children's Court effectively operates an *assembly site* for an array of assessments supplied to it about maladjusted children and their families—*not* a judicial site for testing evidence. This has the effect of marginalising the importance of legal categories of crime while simultaneously placing the agents of the court in a position of considerable strategic influence over the court's decision-making processes. The focus of the Children's Court moves away from determinations about legal responsibility (that is guilt and fault) with regard to a specific offence and assumes the role of a normalising agency itself. This has considerably enlarged the strategic conditions of possibility for dealing with children brought before the courts and, more importantly, has allowed the courts to deal with welfare cases in the same way as juvenile offenders.

There is an important exception. A small proportion of cases (less than 5 per cent) are contested and do require the adjudication of guilt or innocence. I sat through several such cases, all of which invoked the formalism of the legal process ordinarily involved in the hearing and testing of evidence in an adversarial context. But even here in the disposition of contested cases court room discourse shifted between apparently opposing discourses of justice and welfare without contradiction. Judgements about what to do with a child before the court can slide back, forth and between strictly legal considerations about evidence to considerations about the manner, character and family of the child, as they did in many of the cases discussed in the previous chapters and even in contested cases, although to a much lesser extent.

While the Children's Court is often perceived as the fulcrum of the legal process around which all other decision-making processes revolve, such a view is an idealised one, which sets up a hierarchy of decision-making functions with the court at the top. For the reasons set out above, to construe the Children's Court as either the *centre* or *top* of the process vastly over-estimates the importance of judicial forms of decision-making while simultaneously under-rating the role of the agencies which surround the court in that decision-making. In most cases the traditional judicial logic of the penalty tariff is dissolved in favour of a decision-making grid which incorporates social work as a mode of inquiry and psychology as a form of calculus. Three major consequences flow from this, all of which contribute in some way to the blurring of delinquency with neglect. The first is that by reducing the function of the Children's Court to an administrative role, the dispersion of judicial power to the experts has elevated their discretion in making decisions about how to sentence children. A second major consequence is that the focus of the court proceedings shifts from considerations about the nature of the offence to the nature of the individual child before the court. And a final major consequence is that the disposition of a case (whether welfare or criminal) has become dependent on forms of knowledge in which it is not necessary to separate welfare cases from criminal matters. I have called these deficit discourses. These three effects of the dispersion of judicial power are now considered in turn.

Decentring of decision-making

The alliance between judicial, welfare and other administrative agencies in the organisation of juvenile justice has decentred the decision-making processes, such that the court is only one of the important loci of decision making. What this means is that the field of juvenile justice intervention is enlarged well beyond a concern with discrete criminal or delinquent conduct. It also means that agents of the court—psychologists and social workers, for example—become *de facto* 'judges'. They are the gate-keepers to the system. They decide who will be diverted from the legal process and who will not, and what punishment, if any, should be administered. These decisions commonly rest on assessments of the *family* of the child before the court (see Chapter 4) and are presented to the court for authorisation in the form of scientific and expert knowledge contained in court reports, home background reports, psychological tests, records of interview and so on, as the specific cases discussed in this book have documented. At this point in the process, background reports (also referred to as social inquiry reports) prepared by non-legal personnel play a major and, in many cases the major, role in determining court outcomes.

The parents and children who are the objects of these reports, inquiries and proceedings have few means of contesting their substance. There are several reasons for this. The first is that the defendant is nearly always in a position of considerable disadvantage in relation to the crown's investigative resources. Another is that there is no legislative responsibility for defendants and their families to either have access to such documents or even any knowledge of their existence.[2] Even if defendants had both the desired resources and access to these documents, their substance would still be difficult to contest. This is because such documents assume an uncontestable status as truth being written authoritatively 'in the best interests of the child' and generally not as 'the Crown's case'. The most visible end in this process—the court—is, in most cases, little more than a theatrical display which performs a rhetorical, rubber-stamping role. It rarely contests the recommendations put before it by the experts simply because it is rarely in a strategic position to do so. Magistrates do not visit the home and school of the child, or know of his/her background, family, friends, attitudes, manner and likelihood of 're-offending'. They are not in possession of the knowledge required to make an order appropriate to the individual child before the court.

The dispersion of judicial power to the agents that surround the court is most clearly evident in the discretion they exert over the dispositional stage of decision making. The relaxation of formal evidentiary rules permits extra-judicial agencies a great deal of latitude to intervene in the adjudication process and to offer their assessments about how best to manage the child before the court. Several empirical observations provide crucial support for this argument. The first of these is that, in most cases, district officers get the order they request from the presiding magistrate. In relation to the case study sample, 98 per cent of the Children's Court Orders[3] corresponded with the recommendations put before the court by the departmental staff delegated to investigate the child's background and prepare a report for court. A comparative study of decision making in Sydney Children's Courts conducted in the mid-1970s falls within the period of my own frame of research and relates to the same courts. The study reported a similar empirical finding that, in most cases, magistrates' orders agreed with district officers' recommendations and that there was a statistically significant relationship between their decisions (Gamble, 1976, p. 203). However, this is where the agreement ends. The author of this study argues that this does not mean that magistrates merely follow the advice of the court's ancillaries. Rather that district officers recommend the order most acceptable to the magistrate, and this the author suggests is not influenced by the diagnosed needs of the child, but by the previous number of court appearances (Gamble, 1976, p. 204). In other words it is suggested that judicial logic overrides that of welfare in the dispositional stage of the process. However, such an inference can hardly be sustained given the contrary patterns of sentencing produced by the same courts over that period.

This is where a second empirical observation is crucial to this argument. If judicial logic was the driving force behind the sentencing of children by the Children's Courts then the proportion of girls in my random sample committed to institutions should have risen dramatically with consecutive court appearances and the proportion admonished should have almost ceased after one or two court appearances. In addition to this, those who should have received the most harsh penalties should have been girls appearing before the courts for criminal matters and not as 'welfare cases'. None of these sentencing patterns were born out by the patterns of penalties received by the 1046 girls in the random sample. The proportion of custodial outcomes and probation orders actually *declined* for subsequent court appearances, while the proportion of those admonished remained constant (around 10 per cent) for girls appearing before the court as many as eight times (Fig. 7.1). The girls most likely to receive a custodial penalty were not those appearing in court for criminal offences but those appearing for welfare matters (Table 7.1).

How do girls who have not committed any criminal offence come to be the cohort most severely punished by the Children's Courts? 'Pure' judicial logic certainly does not give rise to this pattern of decision making, but the logic of preventative intervention (which infuses judicial with welfare logic) does. That logic prescribes a range of interventions *prior* to the commission of any identifiable offending behaviour. The role of the district officer and departmental psychologist in all this is to identify the predelinquent and channel them into the clutches of the judicial authorities *before* they commit an offence. A range of deficit discourses are utilised in the identification of what is referred to in official discourse as 'predelinquency'. These are discussed in detail later. The relevant point here is that classification as predelinquent is all that is necessary to justify the committal of welfare cases, such as Judy, to institutions. It is the logic of preventative intervention— to save girls like Cheryl from falling into a life of crime, and girls like Lucy from being a threat to the white community, or those like Christine from ending up like their brothers or sisters, or those like Kathy from a mother who cannot be trusted—which produces the

Figure 7.1 Penalty by number of previous offences

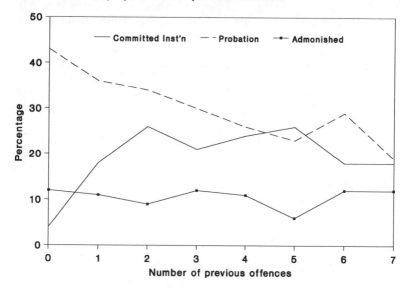

Source: Random sample of 1046 female records from the Juvenile Criminal Index.

Table 7.1 Offence profile of 1046 girls from random sample, by penalty ordered by the Children's Court

Offence/complaint	Probation	Commit inst'n	Fine	Admonish discharge	Withdrawn	Commit wardship[a]	Other	Total
				Court Order				
Uncontrollable	150	74	–	25	47	21	13	330
Exposed to moral danger	94	18	–	19	13	6	8	158
Neglect	53	12	–	4	4	17	9	99
Incompetent guardianship	27	3	–	3	2	57	6	98
Breach of probation	23	53	1	3	5	7	5	97
Abscond	6	15	–	5	5	–	28	59
Destitute (NFPA)	13	1	–	3	1	38	5	61
Other welfare complaints	20	2	–	4	2	1	2	31
Total welfare matters	386	178	1	66	79	147	76	933
Steal	138	25	58	61	9	1	15	307
Fare evasion	–	–	92	18	7	–	1	118
Traffic offences	7	–	64	12	2	–	6	91
Break, enter and steal	44	11	4	4	6	2	–	71
Drug offences	29	6	5	8	–	1	2	51
Unseemly words	14	3	9	14	3	–	1	44
Assault/assault and rob	13	4	3	2	10	–	6	38
Steal motor vehicle	20	4	–	2	5	1	4	36
Under age on licenced prem.	3	–	26	4	–	–	–	33
Receiving/goods in custody	19	2	3	5	–	–	2	31
Other criminal offences	85	11	36	34	7	3	16	192
Total criminal offences	372	66	300	164	49	8	53	1012
Multiple matters	10	5	–	–	1	3	2	21
Non-offence matters	2	1	–	–	4	1	72	80
Total	770	250	301	230	133	159	203	2046

Note: a Includes 58 committals to the guardianship of community-based child welfare agencies.
Source: Random sample of 1046 female records from the Juvenile Criminal Index.

strange patterns of sentencing described above. This logic emerges out of a form of government which takes the maladjusted child and dysfunctional family as its focus of intervention and seeks their normalisation through forms of assistance tied to forms of penal discipline. It is reducible to neither a judicial logic nor a welfare logic—but emerges out of a set of discursive practices which take the welfare of the child as its stated guiding measure, but then draws that child into the same forms of discipline as juvenile offenders.

In vital respects supervising district officers (whose functions have now been taken over by young offender support officers in juvenile justice, and child protection workers in the area of child welfare) are required to act as multi-functionaries in the administration of juvenile justice and child welfare. On the one hand they are required to act in the best interests of children, in particular to protect them from the excesses of neglectful and abusive parents. On the other hand, they are required also to act as part of a prosecution team in the construction of a case. They are the legal complainants in most welfare cases and some criminal matters. But, irrespective of which agency is bringing the complaint, they are the ones generally asked by the court to carry out the investigation into the home and family background of the child, and who then present this information in a court report recommending what intervention, if any, is required. After the court hearing if supervision has been ordered, they are the ones who are generally required to carry out the order. In many instances then the fate of the child before the court is effectively in the hands of the extra-judicial agent who makes a recommendation to the court based on the logic of preventative intervention. It is no wonder Judy saw 'the welfare' as 'the enemy'. She was right. District officers act simultaneously as agents for the prosecution and agents for the child, recommending to the court the order *they* consider to be in the best interests of that child. What Judy thinks is irrelevant in this process. Her status as a 'child' denies her a legitimate claim to know what is in her best interests. Only the district officer is authorised by the court to know this.

The great difficulty associated with the decentring of decision-making processes is that those with the least accountability located at the least visible end in the administration of justice exercise the most power (Hogg, 1991). This form of governmentality is the curious product of an economy of punishment which has 'humanitarian' concerns, in this case child protection, as its primary objective. While the new legislative framework has gone some way towards separating child welfare from juvenile justice that framework is ultimately discretionary. That discretion, as the cases in this book have documented, is sometimes misguided and often unchecked. So the situation today is not necessarily any better than it was before the proclamation of the new legislation in 1988. Still no mechanisms of accountability have been instituted over the administration of juvenile justice to ensure that the busy but less visible agencies responsible for its implementation are made publicly accountable. That almost 150 children can be taken from their homes in a series of pre-dawn raids authorised by a couple of district officers largely on the basis of prejudice about a religious cult, should be enough to convince any sceptic of the enormity of unchecked power that can be exercised by extra-judicial agents[4] in our system of juvenile justice and child welfare.

Individualised judgements

Because the primary function of the Children's Court is to determine outcomes and not guilt, the traditional judicial focus on the *offence* is displaced by a focus on the *individual*, and his/her family background, schooling, leisure activities, peers and so on. Individualised judgements are supplied to the court by its agents, usually in the form of court reports and/or psychological assessments. This book has quoted extensively from such documents. The main purpose of the court report is to provide background information about the individual child before the court; the object of judgement is not the commission of a discrete delinquent act, but the individual before the court and her family background.

Individualised judgements have the effect of marginalising the legal categories under which children are brought before the court. Consequently, it does not much matter whether the conduct was running away from an abusive family, truanting from school, stealing five cents or robbing a bank. The fact that the court sees itself as acting in the best interests of the child, irrespective of how that child ended up before the court, adds to the marginalisation of legal categories in the disposition of specific cases.

Where the matter that comes before the court is in the form of a welfare complaint rather than a criminal matter, the legal categories in question (such as being uncontrollable or neglected under the former legislation or abused and in need of care under the new legislation) are extremely vague and flexible. In the absence of a precise legal standard any range of conduct can be brought before the court under such indiscriminate legal categories. The process is not much different in criminal matters that proceed by way of a guilty plea (which is most of them). Irrespective of whether the case brought before the Children's Court involves a welfare complaint or criminal matter the alleged commission of an offence merely provides the occasion to conduct a wider inquiry into the background of the child before the court, to determine whether the child needs normalising intervention and, if so, what kind. A range of experts are called upon by the court to carry out this function in the disposition of a case. In the cases discussed in this book it was predominantly departmental district officers and psychologists who carried out these extra-judicial duties. Occasionally, educative agents such as school counsellors and school teachers were also called upon to provide knowledge crucial to finding a punishment suited to the child before the court. The forms those knowledges take are the object of analysis in the following section.

One of the bizarre consequences of the individualisation of judgements is, in fact, its opposite—the homogenisation of all children before the courts into a unitary category of maladjusted youth in need of prescribed treatment of one kind or another. We see here not the opposition of two discourses, but the realignment of judicial and welfare discourses into a form of social administration in which is it not necessary to separate neglected from delinquent children. Within such a discourse the delinquent and neglected child are symptomatic of the same problem—a dysfunctional family which has failed to adequately rear, care and educate their offspring.

Deficit discourses

Deciding which order is in 'the best interests of the child' in the disposition of a specific case (whether welfare or criminal) is dependent on knowledge of the individual subject child before the court. The forms of knowledge utilised in deciding this are of three major kinds: inquisitorial, classificatory and interpretative. The home report generally supplies the inquisitorial knowledge about the family and circumstances, the psychological report supplies classificatory knowledge about the nature of the child and his/her family unit, and both reports draw this information into an interpretative assessment about the most appropriate means to administer to the child before the court (Donzelot, 1979). Court reports also generally offer an explanation for the peculiar 'deficiencies' in the individual child and his/her upbringing before the court. By making individual children and their families responsible for acts of truancy, predelinquency or family misfortune the rationale is then provided for tutelary intervention which has as its point of disciplinary application the body of the child before the court. This is why deficit discourses are absolutely crucial in the administration of juvenile justice.

I have chosen a few examples from my research to illustrate how deficit discourses work in the identification of 'problem children' and the management of 'dysfunctional families'. The first looks at their application in locating the blame for truancy with individual children and their families, the second in criminalising cultural difference and social marginality, and the third at the effects of translating family poverty into evidence of family pathology.

At the age of thirteen years, Terry was brought before the Children's Court for failing to attend school. The court was told that, despite being of above average intelligence, Terry was an under-achiever at school and that 'she hates school' (Court Report, 21 September 1978). The psychologist who assessed Terry attributed her dislike of school to being 'totally unmotivated' and her failure at school to the fact that she subscribed to 'anti-authority attitudes' and resented 'efforts made to control her behaviour either at home, at school, or in court' (Psychological Report, 21 September 1978). The magistrate asked the district officer present in court whether she had 'any idea what might spark her dislike of school' (Court Transcripts, 21 September 1978). Instead of answering the question the district officer replied, 'I thought she would be better put in a situation where she didn't have the choice of going to school or not' (Court Transcripts, 21 September 1978). The magistrate then inquired, 'You don't think the situation may exist outside those circumstances which might encourage her to achieve, use all her ability?', to which the district officer replied 'No' (Court Transcripts, 21 September 1979). By making Terry shoulder the blame for her dislike of school, the overly punitive course of action recommended by the district officer thus appears to be the most appropriate to administer in this case. In other words, deficit discourses provide the justice authorities with explanations commensurate with the techniques of punishment delivered by the courts.

By locating the problem as something peculiar to Terry and her family background, truancy is conveniently disconnected from the social relations and specific contexts which shape the experience of schooling. Truancy is instead attributed to individual failure and family malfunction. The translation of truancy into a legal discourse (under Section 72(o)) then provides the legislative basis for punitive kinds of juvenile justice intervention in dealing with truants. Discourses which locate the source of difficulty in the deficit group thus absolve any social responsibility for shaping the kinds of cultural responses to schooling in question. Deficit discourses simply erase fundamental issues about the politics of pedagogy, the institutionalised forms of sexism and racism in schools, and the irrationality of dealing with truancy and other forms of resistance to schooling through judicial mechanisms. They divert attention from the forms of social administration required of schools to deal much more *positively* with resistance to schooling through the organisation of the school day and the re-organisation of curriculum content more generally. These important issues are simply bypassed through the invocation of deficit discourses which attribute all blame to the body of the errant student.

A second example chosen to illustrate the application of deficit discourses in the administration of juvenile justice concerns the translation of cultural difference and social marginality into evidence of 'predelinquency'. Because pathology is assessed in these discourses as deviations from the norm (Rose, 1984, p. 123), for example in relation to normal family size, income and concern about hygiene and education, normal IQ and literacy levels, attitudes to authority, work, school and so on, categories of pathology tend to be diagnosed in the image of the other. So despite the disavowal of race and other forms of prejudice as the grounds for modern day child welfare intervention, deficit discourses provide the welfare authorities with cultural and psychological constructions of normality which continue to have a specifically criminalising effect on socially marginal populations within the social body. The most obvious example of this in the Australian context is the massive criminalisation rates of Aboriginal youth and their families. The psychological report quoted below presents a particularly striking example of deficit discourses at work in providing the justice system with a technique of evaluation which effectively pathologises cultural difference, in this case Aboriginality, and then provides the rationale necessary for severely punishing the Aboriginal girl before the court.

> Sally was seen twice at the remand shelter . . . She presented as a tall, thin, insecure aboriginal [*sic*] girl who was reluctant to talk about her family. She says she is one of eighteen children, . . .
> Sally has lived her whole childhood on the reserve and thus has developed the inner instincts of survival but is lacking social awareness.
> Cognitive testing indicates her to be in the mentally retarded group. However educational factors and cultural factors and lack of social (urban) stimulation would have effected [*sic*] the scores. Verbal tests indicate her to be educationally retarded. On performance tests she is poor in visual–motor areas especially of the spatial nature . . . Sally presents as functioning on an upper borderline low dull normal level.
> Sally is unmotivated to achieve and has poor resistence [*sic*]. She is functioning at present in a basic concrete level where she seeks gratification of her primary needs. She has few behavioural controls and has little value of other's property. She lacks concepts of time, finance, and maintaining social relationships. She is happy with her egocentric lifestyle and reacts strongly when the stability of this is

threatened. Thus counselling will be of little help to this girl both because of her mental functioning and her motivation. . . . Recommend training to continue. (Psychological Report, 6 February 1979)

Sally's crimes may have been trivial, four convictions for drunkenness and one for unseemly words, but her punishment was anything but trivial. At the time of Sally's committal, most juveniles committed to institutions in New South Wales were, like Sally, sentenced in general terms. She spent four-and-half months in a detention centre where she was subjected to the usual forms of psychological evaluation. It is in the context of the general committal that psychological discourses take on a particularly important practical dimension in the administration of juvenile justice. Psychologists recommend that training either continue or that the inmate be discharged. The psychological assessment quoted above clearly endorses Sally's continued institutionalisation on the basis that she has not responded well to training. It is Sally's cultural differences in regard to concepts of time, finance and disregard for private property which effectively provide the bureaucratic rationale for her continued training. Her cultural differences are represented in this psychological discourse not only as deviations, but also as obstacles to her training and normalisation—to the voluntaristic and individualised solutions imposed by judicial and extra-judicial agencies to the visibility of her marginality on the streets of Bourke.

Sally's case was not an isolated or exaggerated example where psychological forms of knowledge performed a crucial role in attributing a range of deficits to Aboriginal girls and which then had a considerable impact on their management in the administration of justice. I want to recount briefly the demonstrable effects of deficit discourses in the decisions affecting Terese's management within the system. After being made a State ward, Terese was temporarily placed in a shelter where she could be assessed. The purpose of this assessment was to decide whether she was suitable for fostering, a family group home, a ward establishment or some other placement. The document has been reproduced almost in its entirety below.

Reason for Admission: BOP (Uncontrollable 7 April 1979)
Last School: Walgett High School OA Class
Test Results: mildly retarded range: 62, 57, 56
Reading age—7 yr 10 m Maths: Simple addition, minus and multiplication
Comments: Terese's recent test results generally placed her abilities in the upper half of the mildly retarded range of intelligence . . .
Her human figure drawing is very immature in concept and quality, reflecting her below average ability and poor body concept

development. Terese's reading and number work skills are
consequently quite limited too. Terese would seem to able to cope
with pure routine manual kind of employment.
Report: Terese was seen following her committal to State care. She
presents as an amiable soft spoken attractive part aboriginal [*sic*]
lass who relates fairly well to the tester. Although Terese was
co-operative in testing, her manners suggested poor motivation and
generally low drive for doing well. When asked about any
misbehaviour Terese was puzzled and denied this. She impressed as
having limited awareness of the implications of her sexual
misconduct and thus seemed quite vulnerable on this aspect . . .
Assessment on some aspects of her social skill acquisition revealed
the following findings which may be compared and supplemented
with the cottage report. Terese reported that her table habit has
improved (with the help of staff at the cottage) since her admittance
approximately 4–5 weeks ago. She seems to be fairly able to look
after her personal hygiene adequately in matters such as having her
hair trimmed . . . Although Terese found little difficulty in getting
around her previous placement, Sydney would clearly present as a
much more complicated area to cover. She will definitely need a lot
of help in this, but there are signs that the girl is 'trainable'. . .
Overall, due to her immaturity and lack of training the girl may
need considerable help on the onset of her working life. However,
with active training and sympathetic interest from adults, Terese
should be able to carry out simple work situations in the open
community. Recommend Placement in Ward Hostel for girls
(Psychological Report, 13 November 1979)

Deficit discourses are not the sole domain of psychological
assessments. Consider, for example, the following report about
Terese after the above placement failed. The report was authored
by a child health counsellor to whom Terese was referred for
assessment by her supervising district officer.

Presentation: Terese presented as an attractive quiet aboriginal [*sic*]
girl, who appeared to be older than her 16 years. She is anxious to
leave school and seek employment, but has little idea of what else
she is interested in. Her extra-curricular activities revolve around
basketball on Saturday mornings, television, looking after her
sister's children, and occasionally going to the pictures with friends.
Academic Record: 3rd form OA level—Her teachers are concerned
that the present level of work may be beyond her capacities and
have suggested she join the workforce. On the day of her court
appearance aged 13.4 years, Terese was given a Weschler
Intelligence scale for children and her full IQ was scored at 56. This
intelligence quotient places her in the mildly retarded range of
intelligence. A reading test administered at the same time gave her a
reading score of 7.3 years, despite her chronological age of 13.4
years.

Conclusion: At this stage because of cognitive and developmental factors, it would appear that Terese is workshop material.
Recommend: Placement in sheltered workshop. (1 February 1980)

On the basis of this report Terese was sent to a sheltered workshop where she remained one week before absconding. Upon being apprehended she was placed on remand in a departmental shelter for girls in Western Sydney. In referring her for psychiatric counselling the social worker attached to that shelter made the following assessment.

> Terese presents as a shy, softly spoken, attractive girl. She does not see herself as being intellectually handicapped. For despite her limited intelligence, Terese is quite practiced at travelling about the country side to visit her relatives and friends. Placement in a hostel and sheltered workshop situation, in the country area, appears to be Terese's most pressing need at this time. (Referral to Westmead Psychiatric Hospital, 22 April 1980)

In all the reports quoted above an array of deficit discourses were utilised, some moral, some psychological, some social, most prejudicial and others legal in coming to an assessment about an individual girl. The important point is that these assessments then had *practical* effects on the way the girls were chosen, placed and punished by the juvenile justice and child welfare authorities. Sally, for example, was classified as 'functioning on an upper borderline low dull normal level' while Terese was considered to be 'workshop material'. These assessments then led to the recommendation that Sally's incarceration continue and that Terese be sent to a sheltered workshop. Because pathology is calculated in these discourses as deviations from the specificity of the norm they have a particularly intense criminalising effect on social marginality. At least some of the vulnerability of Aboriginal girls to criminalisation can be attributed to the forms of knowledge utilised in the administration of juvenile justice. Those forms of knowledge enlist deficit discourses as the means through which predelinquent children and dysfunctional families are identified and managed. The forms of psychological knowledge which service the administration of juvenile justice then provide the rationale for individualised solutions to the 'problems' posed by social marginality and its visibility. For Sally this meant that she had to be locked up and taught the rudimentary skills of hygiene and contraception. For Terese this meant that she had to be sent to a sheltered workshop to be managed alongside others who were classified as intellectually deficient.

The effects of deficit discourses have consequences far beyond the administration of juvenile justice. Here is where this third example of the use of deficit discourses in translating poverty into family pathology is relevant. Deficit discourses extrapolate notions of normality, not from the assessment of 'normal' children, but from evaluations of defective children and families (Rose, 1989, p. 123). Images of the good family produced by expert evaluations of normality then serve as a standard by which defective children and their families sometimes even come to see themselves, evaluate their lives and the conduct of their children (Rose, 1989, p. 130). The following document suggests how this form of governmentality can work through the influence of one family member. Mr Drake, the patriarchal 'head' of an officially classified defective family, had come to define himself and other members of his poverty stricken family in terms similar to those assessing them as dysfunctional. The consequences of this fell mostly on his wife to perform her housewifely duties in a way desired by 'the welfare', but which were not possible because of economic stringencies and other factors such as his own alcoholism. The document was written by a district officer in the context of Mr and Mrs Drake applying for the restoration of their daughter, Maree, several years after she had been removed from their care on the basis that the family was destitute.

> Mr Drake is a truck driver. He seems to be the backbone of the family, managing finance, housekeeping and doing the shopping. Mr Drake is short in stature, low–normal intelligence and poorly spoken. He persisted in telling me that as long as they had the correct number of bedrooms, a permanent address, and wife/mother then Maree could return! If she does not Mr Drake will contact his local member of parliament . . . Mr Drake is trying to play the role of the 'perfect' father to John, making sure that he attends school regularly, does his homework, and saves some of the money he earns from his paper round. He says that he does not drink as much as he used too [sic], however, lately Mrs Drake has accused him of drinking more than 'a few' beers at the weekend. Mr Drake seems to spend most of his time trying to make his wife and son behave in the way 'the welfare' expects a good family to behave . . . Mrs Drake says that she is made to scrub at the clothes untill [sic] her knuckles are red and raw because her husband will not buy a machine but insists that a good family must have white sheets . . .
> *Recommendation*: That Maree is not returned to her parents.
> (Application for Restoration, 22 January 1977)

Deficit discourses are absolutely essential in the administration of juvenile justice. They provide the authorities with the means of predicting and classifying which families are incompetent at rearing children and which children are likely to lapse into a life of vice and crime. Deficit discourses also provide the means for managing such families normalisation when they do. By locating the source of pathology either in a defective individual or dysfunctional family, the rationale is then provided for preventative intervention which works through the restraint of the body of the child (through their being placed in incarceration, on probation or in State care). That intervention, while often experienced as punitive, is usually conceived in terms of benevolence, as the welfare acting in the best interests of the child. This is the issue to which I now turn.

Punishment and welfare

While the child welfare system represents itself as operating in the child's best interests, the question which arises in all this is whether this avowedly benevolent process is experienced as such by those who pass through it. The empirical evidence upon which this book is based overwhelming suggests the contrary. How can one deny that welfare intervention has nothing to do with the operation of repressive power when girls such as Terry were taken to court for truancy, sent to an institution that made no provision for their education and from which they were released with a school exemption. Or when Cheryl, for example, was locked up for her harmless pursuit of fun and pleasure, or, worse still, when Judy was incarcerated by the welfare authorities for running away from a foster family in which she was sexually abused. This girl's need for support was only attainable through her own punishment. One may well ask at this point, how can such cruel and heartless things happen to girls such as Judy who are so obviously victims and not offenders? How can a child welfare system which aims to help girls who are victims of sexual assault actually channel them into detention centres? The short answer is that the fusion between welfare and punishment has made such dispositions possible within the ambit of 'the welfare' acting 'in her best interests, your honour'. The long answer . . . follows.

The fast track from care to detention

The alliance between justice and welfare has channelled many female State wards into detention centres. How the nexus between welfare and justice works can be grasped more clearly if we consider how some of the State wards from this sample were drawn along the fast track from care to detention. Of the fifty-nine girls whose records I examined thirty-six were wards—the vast majority of whom were taken into care well before they were taken into detention. Kay was one of these girls. She was taken into care at the age of twelve years and committed to an institution by the time she was fourteen years of age for assault and malicious injury to government property. The charges arose out of an incident that occurred at the breakfast table in a ward establishment. Kay threw a piece of toast at the house-parent of the ward establishment which also hit the kitchen wall of the ward shelter. Later that day she appeared before the Children's Court charged with assault and malicious injury to government property. More often, however, State wards end up in juvenile institutions for absconding from departmental establishments, as Kathy had done.[5] Indeed, one third of the female wards in my study ended up in detention centres for absconding. In many of these cases the girls (for example Terese (see Chapter 3) and Kathy (Chapter 5)) were simply trying to return to families from whom the department had taken them. By now it should be clear that this child-saving strategy has fallen heavily on families from Aboriginal communities and housing commission estates. It is their children who are driven along the fast track from care to detention.

Once in the hands of the department children convicted of a criminal offence and those placed 'in care' in the past have been, and continue to be, frequently dealt with in identical or similar ways. The girls whose case histories comprise the basis of this book, for example, were sent to the same or similar institutions, the same remand shelters, dealt with by the same personnel and procedures and appeared in the same courts before the same magistrates. Added to this was a considerable traffic of the same bodies between ward establishments and juvenile detention centres. Girls who had nowhere to go after their period of committal were often shipped to ward establishments. Or the other way round, girls who abscond or 'act out' in ward hostels may be sent to detention centres for 'training', as had happened to Kay. On other occasions girls who were considered to be too young for institutionalisation were made State wards instead. This happened to four girls from the case history sample, including Christine Neaves whose case was discussed in Chapter 4.

For those unfamiliar with the juvenile justice system in New South Wales it is important to understand that there are two major avenues through which children and young people may be brought before a Children's Court. On the one hand, children who have reached the age of criminal responsibility (usually ten years old) may be charged with a criminal offence in much the same way as adults. On the other hand, children of any age (usually up to eighteen years) may be brought before the court on what are commonly referred to these days as care matters, but are also known as welfare matters or status offences (such as neglect, abuse, destitution, uncontrollability, truancy and so on). Despite the distinction between criminal grounds and ostensibly protective grounds for coercive intervention in the lives of children, the manner in which they have been processed through the Children's Courts and managed in institutional forms of care and control have not been clearly differentiated. In many cases children before the courts for their own protection are detained in the same institutions as juvenile offenders. In any case the use of separate institutions for children in need of protection (that is, State ward establishments) does not mean that these institutions differ significantly from juvenile prisons in their level of internal security and organisation of their internal daily regime (see illustrations on pp 132 and 133.).

The sentencing powers provided by the *Child Welfare Act* 1939 (NSW) to deal with welfare matters and criminal offences were set out in the same part of the Act and were almost identical for neglected and uncontrollable children (under Section 82), those charged with a criminal offence (under Section 83.1) and those convicted of an indictable offence (under Section 83.2). These legislative provisions have allowed the Children's Court to commit a neglected or uncontrollable child to an institution or vice versa, to commit to wardship a child before the court for a criminal offence and to place both on probation. Of the fifty-nine girls in the case history study, for example, fifty-eight of their court appearances for welfare matters resulted in the court ordering their committal to an institution, and three of their appearances for criminal offences ended up in their being made State wards (Table 7.2).

The 1987 legislative framework has provided for a much clearer separation of care from criminal matters, with the sentencing powers in relation to each being set out in entirely different Acts. However *The Children (Care and Protection) Act* 1987 falls short of making that separation mandatory. Section 18 of that Act only requires that they be accommodated separately 'so far as is reasonably practical'. The responsibility for effecting that separation falls into the hands of those with the administrative discretion in the system, once again those who operate in the least visible aspects of that system— placement officers, district officers and psychologists. This is why it did not matter that Terry, although committed to a training school for truants, was placed in a detention centre. It did not even matter when she appealed to the District Court for, ultimately, placement within the system is discretionary, even under the new legislation.

The department itself has been absolutely frank about collapsing delinquent and neglected children into one undifferentiated category. In the official history of child welfare in NSW the uncontrollable child is even described as having a certain affinity with the delinquent child 'in that the conduct of both is socially unacceptable, and prima facie at least, is deliberate, hence the tendency for them to be treated similarly' (New South Wales Child Welfare and Social Welfare Department, 1970, p. 26). When the forms of social administration for dealing with welfare cases are similar, and share

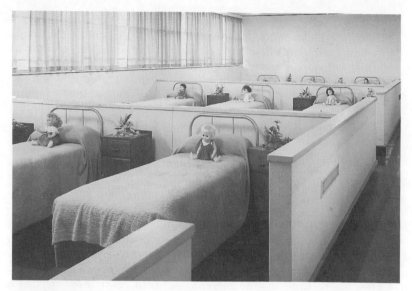

One of the dorms at Brush Farm, *formerly a residential care unit for State wards. (Reproduced with kind permission of N.S.W. Department of Community Services.)*

A girls' dorm at Reiby, *a juvenile detention centre. (Reproduced with kind permission of N.S.W. Department of Community Services.)*

Anglewood, *formerly a training school for truants, recently a residential care unit for wards, (sold in 1993). (Reproduced with kind permission of N.S.W. Department of Community Services.)*

Parramatta Girls Training School, *formerly a juvenile detention centre. (Reproduced with kind permission of N.S.W. Department of Community Services.)*

Table 7.2 Offence profile of the 59 girls from case study, by penalty ordered by the Children's Court[a].

Offence/complaint	Probation	Commit inst'n	Court Order			Commit wardship	Other	Total
			Fine	Admonish discharge	Withdrawn			
Uncontrollable/EMD	28	24	–	–	11	14	2	79
Abscond	3	12	–	3	2	1	17	38
Neglect/incompetent guard'ship	6	1	–	–	1	23	1	32
Breach of probation	1	14	–	–	–	3	1	19
Truancy	6	7	–	–	–	1	1	15
Public mischief	–	–	–	–	–	1	–	1
Insubordination	–	–	–	1	–	–	–	1
Total welfare matters	44	58	0	4	14	43	22	185
Steal	7	8	1	–	–	1	3	20
Break, enter and steal	4	9	–	2	1	2	2	20
Steal motor vehicle	2	5	–	1	2	–	1	11
Drug offences	1	1	–	–	–	–	3	5
Alcohol related offences	2	–	1	1	–	–	–	5
Assault/assault and rob	–	–	–	–	3	–	1	4
Malicious injury	1	1	1	–	–	–	–	4
Driving offences	–	–	2	–	–	–	–	2
Prostitution	1	1	–	1	–	–	–	2
Unseemly words	–	–	–	–	–	–	1	2
Larceny as servant	–	–	–	–	–	–	1	1
Steal m/v, assault and rob	–	1	–	–	–	–	–	1
Total criminal offences	18	27	5	5	6	3	13	77
Total	62	85	5	9	20	46	35	262

Note: [a] Excludes 25 appeals to the District Court—all were dismissed.
Source: Data derived from methodology explained in Chapter 1 (see pp. 4–8).

a similar genealogy to the forms of knowledge essential to the classification of predelinquency, it should be no surprise they are treated in like fashion.

Child welfare and juvenile justice have never constituted wholly separate domains in a formal legal sense, let alone in their day-to-day administration. While recent reforms have attempted to separate welfare from criminal cases the nexus between the two still exists because the mundane daily management of the abused child and the abusive child largely rely on similar forms of administration.

In her best interests your honour: court outcomes

Before turning 18 years of age, the 1046 girls whose records comprised the basis of the statistical sample appeared before the court 2046 times. Their appearances were almost equally divided between welfare and criminal matters (46 per cent of their appearances involved welfare matters, 49 per cent criminal offences and 5 per cent miscellaneous reasons including appeals). In order of highest frequency the following offences account for most of the court action against the 1046 girls: being uncontrollable (16 per cent), stealing (15 per cent), being neglected or under improper guardianship (10 per cent), being exposed to moral danger (8 per cent), fare evasion (6 per cent), breaching probation (5 per cent), traffic related offences (4.5 per cent), break, enter and steal (3.5 per cent) and absconding from custody (3 per cent). This list of offences suggests that the girls in the sample rarely posed a threat to community sufficient to warrant their exclusion from it through incarceration. Yet 19 per cent of the girls appearing before the court on welfare complaints were committed to corrective institutions compared with 6 per cent of those appearing on criminal charges. Only 12 per cent (130) of 1046 girls were admonished and discharged as a result of their very first court appearance. Nearly half (445 of the 1046 girls) were placed on probation and thirty-seven girls were even committed to an institution for their first offence (Table 7.1).

There are three important points to be drawn from the description of the offence/sentencing profile of the 1046 girls. The first is that their high rate of committal to detention is inexplicable in terms of the logic of proportional sentencing. Very few offences committed by girls were serious or involved violence or represented any threat to the community. For reasons previously outlined it is the logic of preventative intervention that has given rise to the harsh penalties handed down to the girls in this sample. A second and related point is that it is nonsense to suggest that juvenile justice 'goes soft' on young offenders or lets most first offenders 'off the hook'. Many of these girls were incarcerated for non-criminal offences and for conduct as petty as bed-wetting, smoking, truanting, running away from home, absconding from ward hostels, breaching probation, staying out late at night, shop-lifting and hanging around the streets. Most of this is conduct for which court action cannot even be taken against adults. Because the object of concern shifts in the criminalisation process from the offence to the individual, these girls were not being punished for their 'crimes', but for their social marginality and, in particular for the failure of their families to be in a position to adequately provide the education, support and encouragement expected by the welfare authorities and other family technicians.

A third point about the offending profile of the 1046 girls concerns the discrepancy between the punishment of first offenders and 'repeat' offenders. Only after going hard on young offenders for their initial court appearances, and institutionalisation having failed as a deterrent, do the authorities then turn to less punitive measures. So the system works in the reverse way to the way in which it is commonly perceived. First and second time offenders generally 'get it tough', and are rarely 'let off the hook', while repeat offenders are increasingly more likely to receive lenient sentences (Figure 7.1).

Once girls are committed to an institution (or ward establishment) this punishment carries with it not only the deprivation of liberty but also a range of carceral disciplines such as the routine censure of mail, restriction on visitors, and use of punishments such as solitary confinement. The documents recorded little of the daily routine of juvenile detention centres and ward establishments, but what there was suggested that discipline within them was despotic, petty and unceasing. Kathy Jones, for example, was sent down a section for tattooing. Freda was placed in solitary confinement for twenty-four hours for calling one of the officers 'a fucking cunt'. On a separate occasion this girl was sent to solitary for smoking. Debbie Herford was placed in solitary for refusing to pick up an orange peel dropped by an officer and for then swearing at that officer's request. Maree Drake was placed in isolation to work for one week after mucking up in class. Sally Cole was sent into solitary for swearing. Cheryl Smales lost privileges for one week after attempting an escape. This meant all her personal belongings and clothes were withdrawn. She literally had to wear the stigma of punishment in the form of a baggy blue uniform. When caught with a pair of jeans hidden under her bed officers then threatened to cancel her holiday leave.

What is interesting about this list of transgressions and punishments is that some of these institutions were ward establishments, others training schools and others detention centres. Given that ward establishments seemed to differ little in the way they managed their inmate population, committal to State care as a ward can be experienced as a severe or even more severe penalty than committal to an institution. At least those committed to detention centres have release dates and rarely stay longer than six to twelve months. Those in ward establishments either stay until they are eighteen years or else they abscond. Wardship and incarceration are in vital respects interchangeable forms of punishment.

Quite apart from the concern about the undifferentiated treatment of State wards from juvenile offenders there is an overriding concern with the effects of institutionalisation more generally. The experience of institutionalisation has been widely recognised as having criminogenic and negativistic effects (Asher, 1986, p. xi). Of the forty girls in the case history sample committed to institutions, twenty-eight were subsequently recommitted. Research on the effects of incarceration on juveniles suggests that: it exacerbates antagonism to authority; reduces self-reliance; produces institutional dependency; reinforces delinquency and increases the likelihood of re-offending; leads to stigmatisation and alienation; and produces higher rates of recidivism than non-custodial alternatives (Frieberg, et al 1988, p. 156). The failure of custodial sentencing provided the impetus for a major reorganisation of young offender services in New South Wales in the early 1980s. That reorganisation stressed the need for diversion programs, such as police cautioning and strategies of decarceration, such as the use of community youth centres instead of detention. The department was quite explicit about the reasons for these changes in its 1985 Annual Report.

> The reorganisation was approved following a review of recent research which clearly showed that the committal of young offenders did not inhibit crime but actually reinforced attitudes and behaviour which led to increased criminal activity. (YACS Annual Report, 1985, p. 30)

Incarceration had anything but a rehabilitative effect on Joan, one of the girls whose cases I read. The department itself acknowledges such in the document quoted below. Joan was a recidivist described as 'having youth workers in the way that others have aunts and uncles'. She had been committed to an institution five times over a period of three years. During that time she had become so institutionally dependent that incarceration was no longer perceived as a punishment.

It is extremely difficult to decide what to recommend in a case like Joan's. Her prognosis is extremely poor and she is most unreceptive to any attempts to helping her. She has already spent a considerable amount of time in institutions, and they have been unable to retard the progress of her delinquency. I feel that a further period in such a place would have little or no positive effect in the long term. Joan had recently demanded that she be recommitted but has since agreed to return home if the court permits. (Psychological Assessment for Children's Court, 31 January 1981)

The logic applied in Joan's case is a partial explanation of the weird sentencing outcomes depicted in Figure 7.1. In fact, it was rare for discharge reports to state that institutionalisation had a positive effect on the girl in question. It was more common for these documents to express the opposite view, for example that:

Despite real efforts to help Mary with her problems the programme has so far only been marginally successful. (Recommendation for Release, 24 May 1979)

Despite the widespread acknowledgement of the failure and cost of custodial sentencing this is the path which the current policy regime has chosen. New South Wales has the highest rate of juvenile incarceration in Australia. On the basis of the national arrest rates for juveniles in Australia, it would appear that most of the juveniles who contribute to the high official arrest rates for minor offences in their adolescent years abandon such activities at the onset of adulthood (Mukherjee, 1983). Indeed of the 1046 girls in the random sample over half (51.2 per cent) only appeared once before the Children's Court during their adolescence and 80 per cent were aged between fourteen and eighteen years. Most of their offences were petty and few involved any violence or threat to the community. Hence, to discourage or curtail the use of cautioning or diversion programs for minor offences, as the current government has, makes little policy sense because it heads down the path of committing more public resources to the apprehension, containment and arrest of youth. There is no obvious or necessary social benefit to be gained by locking more and more young people up for petty, trivial offences.

Contesting outcomes

The capacity of girls to contest their treatment by the juvenile justice/welfare authorities was greatly limited given that most were in a position of considerable vulnerability. Nevertheless of the cases I read most did seem to make an effort to resist their punishment by the authorities. Some, for example, appealed against their sentences. Over half the girls from the random sample appealed against their committal to an institution, and twenty-five of the girls in the case history study also lodged appeals against the severity of their sentences. None were successful. Seven appeals, although dismissed did nevertheless result in minor variations to the length and type of order made by the Children's Court (Table 7.3).

While some appealed, others absconded. Half of the girls in the case study cohort had absconded at least once from state custody. Of the thirty-six wards in this cohort, twenty-two absconded a total of eighty-three times from various ward institutions and foster placements. Except for one ward, all were taken to court for absconding and ten girls were incarcerated as a result. After a dozen or so attempts at escaping the most determined of these wards did manage to engineer a successful escape. This was how Judy, whose case has been referred to numerous times throughout the text, ultimately escaped from 'the welfare'. This is also how Terese Hill, taken into State care, sent to a sheltered workshop and then a psychiatric institution, eventually escaped the clutches of the welfare. Kathy Jones whose case you may recall from Chapter 4, also managed a successful reunion with her family after several failed attempts. Girls committed to detention centres were not so successful. Of the fourteen among them who escaped nineteen times, all except one were apprehended and returned to custody and sent down a section lengthening their period of committal.

It seems that parents were better placed strategically to contest the treatment of their daughters by the child welfare and juvenile

Table 7.3 Appeals and other non-offence matters[a]

Non-offence matter	Court Order					
	Harsher penalty	NEOD NBC[b]	Appeal dism'd	Appeal upheld	Order terminated	Total
Appeals to the district court	3	6	55	1	–	65
Application to terminate order	–	2	1	–	9	12
Application for variation of court order	1	1	–	–	1	3
Total	4	9	56	1	10	80

Note: [a] Among the random sample of 1046 girls.
         [b] NEOD—no evidence offered, dismissed.
         NBC–not before court.

Source: Random sample of 1046 female records from the Juvenile Criminal index.

justice authorities. Some parents wrote letters to the director of the department and the relevant Minister. And some parents enlisted the support of their local Members of Parliament to do the same. For example, Mrs Issac's children had been taken into State care at her own behest to protect them from an estranged husband who had threatened to kill the family. Their committal to state care was supposed to be temporary. However, Mrs Issac was later informed that her children would not be returned to her care until she had found employment and appropriate accommodation. Several months later, after fulfilling these requirements, her application for restoration of her children was again declined. The district officer assessing her application felt that the department could provide a better material standard of living for the children, since Mrs Issac would have to resign from her employment and become 'welfare dependent', if the children were returned to her care. Mrs Issac's response was the following letter written to the Minister at the time.

Dear Sir,
I would like to know why my children are not being handed back to me. I put in for them in February for them to be handed back to me but I have just been refused. This is not very good for my children. It must be a big disappointment as they have been waiting to come to me. You people are always saying we dump our children in homes because we don't want them, but I can assure you I very much want my children now why can't I have them. They were only made State Wards to protect them against their father. They were never neglected children or uncontrollable.

Yours Sincerely,
Mrs Issac, May 1980

Recent attempts to remodel juvenile justice

In the late 1970s there was an attempt to remodel the justice system in New South Wales with the drafting of new legislation, the ill-fated *Community Welfare Act* 1982 (NSW). However, the Act was only partially proclaimed and was superseded in 1988 by a package of Acts[6] which replaced the *Child Welfare Act* 1939 (NSW). As previously stated, the new legislative framework was the first in this State's history to clearly separate child welfare provisions from those of juvenile justice. Children coming before the court for welfare matters are now dealt with under the provisions of the *Children (Care and Protection) Act* 1987, while those appearing before the court for criminal matters are dealt with according to the *Children (Criminal Proceedings) Act* 1987.

As already noted the new legislation does differentiate between absconding from a ward shelter and escaping from a detention centre and this may prevent some girls from being driven along the fast track from care to detention. Nevertheless girls with welfare histories (i.e. as care cases or State wards) continue to be channelled into detention centres. Because the number and proportion of girls taken into the system under care/welfare proceedings has dropped significantly in NSW since 1985 (Figure 2.2), it is only logical that if far fewer girls are entering the system as welfare cases then they will constitute a smaller proportion of the total number of girls taken into custody. But none of this has an effect on the proportion of female wards or care cases who, at some stage before turning 18, are moving from care to detention. It could still be as high as 1 in 5. There is just no way of knowing because no comparable data base exists. Indeed one of the major points to emerge from the 1992 Review of Substitute Care Services in NSW, also known as the Usher Report, is how little information the government has about the fate of children who enter the child welfare system in this State. The Usher report identified the lack of adequate data collection charting the progress of children in the system as a major obstacle to planning services (Usher, 1992, p. 15). Mowbray, even suggests that the NSW Government 'is in no position to know something so basic as whether, for example, more or less children have gone into care' (Mowbray, 1992, p. 6).

Prior to the proclamation of the 1987 legislation on 18 January 1988, the formerly named Department of Youth and Community Services had undertaken a series of major administrative reforms with the restructuring of young offenders services (YACS, 1985). The reorganisation introduced new diversion schemes, such as police cautioning, and embarked on a strategy of de-institutionalisation with daily attendance at Community Youth Centres replacing detention for some offenders, a Community Cottage program and centralised Juvenile Justice Unit and the institution of a number of regionally-based Young Offender Support Teams. Simultaneously, the department established a Child Protection Unit, gave up on policing truants and uncontrollables and chose instead to concentrate its resources more intelligently on child abuse and its prevention. Truancy ceased being policed by the department's field division, not when it was removed as an offence in 1988, but in 1985 when the department reorganised its priorities (see Fig. 4.1, Chapter 4). Court action taken against 'uncontrollables' also declined dramatically during the years preceding its removal as a welfare offence under the new legislation (Table 7.4). While the legislative separation of child welfare from juvenile justice is a positive advance on the *Child Welfare Act* 1939, in many respects it simply *followed* the major reforms that had

Table 7.4 Uncontrollable complaints by sex, NSW Children's Courts

Year[a]	Boys	%	Girls	%	Total
1965	223	51	216	49	439
1966	243	50	245	50	488
1967	237	42	327	58	564
1968	240	44	303	56	543
1969	273	47	306	53	579
1970	301	46	362	54	663
1971	282	40	413	60	695
1972	328	39	516	61	844
1973	350	38	579	62	929
1974	428	44	553	56	981
1975	360	39	574	61	934
1976	335	39	517	61	852
1977	258	36	455	64	713
1978	292	41	417	59	709
1979	276	42	376	58	652
1980	264	41	385	59	649
1981	333	44	430	56	763
1982	361	44	451	56	812
1983	—	—	—	—	—[b]
1984	381	51	372	49	753
1985	343	49	358	51	701
1986	199	55	166	45	365
1987	240	51	227	49	467
1988	69	53	61	47	130
1989[c]	5	56	4	44	9

Notes: [a] Data from 1988 onwards relate to proven matters only.
[b] Comparable data unavailable for 1983.
[c] Uncontrollable ceased to be a welfare offence in 1988. The few anomalous
matters for uncontrollable recorded in the Children's Court statistics for the
financial year of 1989 probably relate to the 1988 calendar year.
Source: YACS Annual reports 1965 to 1983, and NSW Bureau of Crime Statistics and
Research for 1984 to 1990.

already occurred in the administration of juvenile justice which were
initiated by the department itself.

Since the election of a more conservative State government many
of these reforms to the juvenile justice system have been dismantled
(Youth Justice Coalition, 1990, pp. 4–6). There have been dramatic
increases in the length of detention, new categories of offences and
increased penalties for behaviour associated with juveniles, for
example the reinstitution of truancy as an offence), a renewed
emphasis on militarism and discipline in detention centres, and
greater numbers of children being transferred to adult prisons (Youth
Justice Coalition, 1990, p. 6).

The maximisation of law enforcement resources and the
intensification of penal measures have been characteristic
dimensions of New Right politics in Australia, and elsewhere, in

recent times. Crime has been located within a discourse which disassociates it from social and economic relations and instead attributes it to the voluntarist and pathological acts of individuals warped by moral decay and family breakdown (Hogg and Brown, 1991). Such a discourse on law and order has shaped the *Summary Offences Act* 1988 (NSW) and the *Sentencing Act* 1989 (NSW) both of which have been passed since the conservative government took office. The latest in this predictable series of developments in the 'get tough' approach has seen the relocation of juvenile justice to the Department of Corrective Services lumping its management in with that of adult prisons. The 'get tough' approach to juvenile offenders is not necessarily confined to States with conservative governments. Western Australia's previous Labor government lowered the age of imprisonment and increased sentences available to the Children's Courts in response to demands for stiffer penalties from a group calling itself the justice lobby(!). The group formed after a series of deaths occurred as a result of car crashes involving police and stolen vehicles. Most of the stolen vehicles were driven by Aboriginal youth. Ten 'innocent bystanders' and six 'offenders' have died in these high-speed car chases. Little has been said about the lunacy of police chasing stolen vehicles at high speeds in built-up areas.

At the same time as stiffening sentences against young offenders the New South Wales government established an upper house standing committee to inquire into juvenile justice.[7] That committee has suggested a mixed bag of recommendations, some of which depart significantly from the rhetoric of law and order politics. Its two most important recommendations include the wider use of police cautioning (recommendations 15–19) and the establishment of children's panels (recommendations 35–50) as methods for diverting many of the trivial forms of conduct that currently come before the courts (Standing Committee on Social Issues, 1992). The committee has also recommended that the position of policy officer (girls) be created within the Office of Juvenile Justice to specifically deal with issues affecting girls and to develop strategies deterring them from entering the juvenile justice system (recommendation 12). While these initiatives are welcome the majority report of the committee failed to recommend either the repeal of the *Summary Offences Act* 1988 or the *Sentencing Act* 1989 both of which are crucial if young people are to be diverted from penal institutions. It also failed to recommend the abandonment of Community Aid Panels, an initiative of the police department which has no legislative mandate. These panels were criticised by the committee, and recently by Dyer M.P. the Shadow Minister for justice in the legislative council (Hansard, 29 October 1992, pp. 41–46), for competing with police cautions, for having a net-widening effect and for dispensing penalties far out of alignment with the petty nature of the offences that come before them. A recent piece of evaluative research has also seriously questioned the usefulness of Community Aid Panels (Bargen, 1992). The NSW Minister for Justice has since released for public comment *The Green Paper: Future Directions for Juvenile Justice in New South Wales* (1993). This document has recommended the amending of the *Sentencing Act* 1989 (NSW), but not the *Summary Offences Act* 1988 (NSW) and has stated a preference for continuing with Community Aid Panels.

What is interesting about both these documents is that they seem to be resurrecting the wisdom of the reforms initiated by the department itself during the 1980s when Frank Walker was the minister without, however, confronting that many of these have been dismantled by the actions of the current government.

In the recent political context public debate has become even more polarised between what one journalist has termed 'the "lock-'em-up" mentality versus the "do-gooder" brigade' (Laurie, 1992, p. 17). For some wishing to reform the justice system, such as concerned parents of Aboriginal youth, support for a welfare model is understandable given that it has been their children disproportionately affected by a 'get tough approach' to juvenile offenders. For others, like the justice lobby, the welfare model, and those seen to be advocating it (referred to locally as the white sand-shoe brigade) have been ridiculed as 'going soft' and 'letting young crims off the hook'.[8] Despite my sympathy for a welfare approach as a political position, the debate about justice versus welfare models of juvenile justice is, as Pratt suggests, 'something of a side show' (Pratt, 1989, p. 250). The major problem with the way in which juvenile justice works, as identified repeatedly in the pages within this text, has been the enduring nexus that exists between welfare and justice and not the way they supposedly operate in contradiction. That nexus has, in the past, robbed families from Aboriginal communities and housing commission areas of their children and then driven many of those same children along the fast track from care to detention. In fact the number of Aboriginal children coming into the hands of the welfare has actually risen in recent years. In 1992 the number of Aboriginal children in care is a staggering 18.8 per cent of all such children (Department of Community Services, 1992), making them over-represented in care by a factor of nine.

Ironically the number of children under care and protection orders in New South Wales has almost halved (from 5183 in 1984 to 2932 in 1990) since child protection became the major focus of the department's activities (Standing Committee of Social Welfare Administrators, 1992, p. 49). Children who formerly would have been made wards are being placed by the department into the care of non-government agencies, bypassing the courts and the necessity to make such children State wards. Indeed wards now comprise only 58 per cent of the children in substitue care compared with 74 per cent in 1987 (Department of Community Services, 1992, p. 3). While placing children under less intrusive forms of care and protection than wardship is, in respects, an advance on placing them in institutions, many children in need of support are being left out of the care system altogether. As Mowbray suggests, the greatest benefit to be derived from such a policy accrues to the state government in the form of fiscal savings (Mowbray, 1992, p. 4).

In the contemporary context it seems more likely that children without adequate family support will no longer come into the justice system as State wards but as street kids through criminal proceedings. This is because there is a great lack of social provision for family-less youth who tend to be homeless, transient tenants in youth refuges. These conditions of marginality then understandably push them into the hands of the police or the welfare authorities often with the effect of compounding their initial marginality. The situation in New South Wales is likely to worsen. This is because the Coalition State government has withdrawn significant sums of money from the forms of support for homeless youth. This government has consistently underspent its budget for the Supported Accommodation Assistance Program (SAAP), by over five million dollars in the 1991 financial year and by eighteen million dollars in the two previous financial years (Dyer, M.L.C., Press Release, 12 November 1992). The SAAP budget is the primary funding source for youth refuges and other forms of accommodation for homeless youth. While these are not entirely satisfactory forms of assistance for homeless youth or State wards, making them so requires increases in expenditure. With the closure of some ward institutions imminent it seems that the State wards who remain in the system will be tipped onto the streets and can expect little by way of income or housing support from the current State government. Underscoring the vast lack of government provision for homeless girls, boys and State wards is the mistaken view that children not in families are not entitled to anything like proper material housing, social and emotional support.

8 Concluding note

> In all circumstances, particularly in view of her attitude, I
> feel that Judy should be committed in general terms where
> efforts can be made in a controlled situation to rectify
> some of the damage that has already been done. (Court
> Report, 10 August 1979)

Girls such as Judy who, through no fault of their own, have little
or no family support are particularly vulnerable to being driven
along the fast track from care to detention. They are no longer
insulated by their 'innocence' or by their families—either because
they do not have a family (or the one they do have is abusive) or
because their family, by being assessed as dysfunctional, is not in
a position to protect them from the disciplinary gaze of the justice
authorities, as is the case with many families from Aboriginal
communities and housing commission areas. Added to this, is the
great lack of social provision for family-less girls who tend to be
homeless, transient tenants in youth refuges or wards of the State
as previously mentioned. These conditions of marginality then
understandably push them into the hands of the police or the welfare
authorities often with the effect of compounding their initial marginality. New offence categories such as 'frequenting a public place'
(Section 60.2 *Children (Care and Protection) Amendment Act*), by
criminalising homelessness does nothing but add to the magnitude
of the problems that homeless girls, and youth more generally,
already encounter in the transition to adulthood.

That one in five female State wards end up in detention at some
stage before turning eighteen is a dreadful indictment on a welfare
system that takes children into care but has, in fact, a long history
of providing very little care. This issue has been considered
numerous times in the pages within. The point worth stressing here
is that any analysis of the effects of juvenile justice is just not
possible without also considering the operation of a child welfare

146

system that channels so many care cases into it. The forms of administration necessary to break this nexus await invention.

It should not be surprising that it is unsupported youth (that is State wards, homeless youth and girls living in incestuous or intolerable family environments) who are the most vulnerable to detection for petty delinquencies. When they are detected for offending behaviour they are much more likely to be sentenced to an institution. Indeed, evidence put before the New South Wales Standing Committee on Juvenile Justice suggested that 'Girls who are State wards are forty times more likely to be detained in custody than other girls. Boys who are State wards are seventeen times more likely to be detained in custody than non-State wards' (Standing Committee on Juvenile Justice, 1992, p. 51).

My main purpose in writing this book has been to examine not how juvenile justice should work but how it does work. How it works jars considerably in vital respects with the rhetoric of benevolence used so often to describe the way in which it operates. One of the major trends in juvenile justice has been the enlargement of possibilities for the social administration of maladjusted youth and dysfunctional families. That discursive enlargement has created an enduring nexus between welfare and punishment extending considerably the prospects for punishing girls who simply transgress the norms of sexuality, femininity and adolescence. Much of this punishment is then left to the discretion of extra-judicial agents to recommend, supervise and administer. Social workers, district officers, psychologists and a range of other educative agents have emerged to undertake the largely unaccountable extra-judicial functions that have necessarily arisen out of the shifts in punishment which have taken the individual and not the offence as its object of correction. The major problem with this method of government is that the exercise of power in the administration of juvenile justice is largely invisible. Those who are most vulnerable to it (mostly Aboriginal girls and girls from housing commission areas) are least able to defend themselves when falsely or zealously accused of delinquency or family dysfunction.

I am not suggesting that the shifts in punishment which have led to the invisibility and dispersion of penalty are necessarily good or bad in every or any instance. Who could possibly suggest that the family, with all its possibilities for incest and child abuse, should remain closed from the scrutiny of the forms of government which encircle it. What I am suggesting is that the dissolution of justice and its fusion with welfare has given rise to new forms of governmentality in the field of justice administration which are largely *punitive* rather than *positive* in their effects. This fusion has de-centred the role of the Children's Court, problematised the role of welfare agencies within it and created an ongoing escalating spiral between welfare and punishment, robbing impoverished families of their children and filling detention centres with children who simply need support. Given that court action is generally only sought in cases considered unresponsive to normalising intervention, these disciplinary processes have had a much wider field of penetration than the actual numbers of children coming before the courts. Juvenile justice therefore constitutes a realm of penality which has a routinised reach into the lives of girls (and presumably boys also) not insulated from it by their families or their schools. This book has considered several cases where this has occurred. Through absolutely no fault of their own many of these girls were then catapulted into the nexus that exists between welfare and justice and driven along the fast track from care to detention. This is how the juvenile justice system is itself capable of manufacturing female delinquency and how unfortunate girls like Judy end up in juvenile detention centres.

Notes

Chapter 2

1 See, for example, the following debates: Allen, 1989; Brown, 1986; Cain, 1986; Carlen, 1985; Carlen, 1992; Dahl, 1986; Daly, 1989; Gelsthorpe, 1986; Harris, 1990; Howe, 1987; MacKinnon, 1983; Smart, 1986; Smart, 1989 and Van Swaaningen, 1989.

2 Judy had the following list of offences recorded against her name in the NSW juvenile criminal index. Dates have been altered slightly and the names of particular Children's Courts and magistrates presiding over those courts have been excluded in the interests of suppressing any individually identifying information.

Date	Matter/offence	Court Order
July 1979	Exposed to moral danger	Probation 12 months
Aug. 1979	Breach of probation	Suspended Committal 18 mths
Oct. 1979	Uncontrollable	Committal to an Institution
Jan. 1980	Uncontrollable	Committal to an Institution
June 1980	Destitute	Committal to Wardship
Jan. 1981	Abscond	Committal to an Institution

3 About one month into her suspended committal a hand-written note on Judy's file stated that she gave evidence in a carnal knowledge matter.

4 Hancock reiterates this argument in a number of subsequent co-authored publications (see, for example, Chesney-Lind and Hancock, 1982, p. 109; Chesney-Lind and Hancock, 1985, p. 236; Hancock and Hiller, 1981, p. 121).

5 Correlations of the detection rates for female delinquency listed in Table 2.1 with Australian Bureau of Statistics socio-economic indices, suggest that the LGAs of Sydney with the highest rates have fewer high income earners (r=−.42) and professionals (r=−.4), more tradespeople (r=.42),

more households classified as impoverished (r=.23) and considerably
more unemployed (r=.67). More details about these correlations can be
found in Carrington, 1989, pp. 135–9.

6 The average ratio of females to males processed by NSW Children's
Courts over the last three decades was one girl to every four to five
boys with a range between 1:3.6 and 1:6.3 (Carrington, 1989, p. 117).

7 This is a point which Hampton argues in relation to girls appearing
before New Zealand Courts for welfare matters (Hampton, 1979, p. 31).

8 There were another fifty-eight case files which I read during the course
of completing the research upon which this book is based.

9 Much of this analysis was originally inspired by a brilliant piece of
innovative intellectual work by Debbie Tyler about 'The death of Irene
Tuckerman' published in 1986.

Chapter 3

1 For a detailed discussion about specific policing strategies in Wilcannia,
see Carrington, 1991a.

2 Lucy is a pseudonym for one of the Aboriginal girls whose criminal
records I examined.

3 In NSW the forcible removal of Aboriginal children has been allowed
to continue this century through the enactment of several pieces of
legislation. The first of these was the *Aborigines Protection Act* 1909.
Sixty years later the *Aborigines Protection Act* 1969 dissolved the
Aborigines Welfare Board and transferred the power to remove Aboriginal children to the *Child Welfare Act* 1939, which was transferred again
in January 1988 to the *Children (Care and Protection) Act* 1987. For
more details see McCorquodale, 1987 and Read, undated, p. 5.

Chapter 4

1 See note 6, Chapter 7 for details of this package of legislation.

Chapter 5

1 In one of the few years for which this kind of information exists, district
officers in the State made a total of 780 449 home visits, inquiries,
inspections and court attendances (Annual Report, 1973, pp. 60–1).
Only 19 164 of these were court-ordered or court-related attendances.

2 The 1981 Census recorded an unemployment rate of 5.6 per cent for
New South Wales. See ABS Catalogue No. 2401.1, p. 78.

3 Welfare dependency rates for the Australian population during this time
were around ten per cent. See M.A. Jones, *Social Welfare in Australia*,
1985, p. 101.

4 Of the fifty-nine families, thirty-one lived in rental accommodation,
which is almost double the proportion of families recorded in the 1981
Census as living in rental accommodation. See ABS Catalogue No.
2401.1, p. 78.

5 Sixteen families rented their premises from the housing commission;

five times the proportion of families in NSW who live in housing commission accommodation. See ABS Catalogue No. 2401.1, p. 78.

6 Court action for absconding from a departmental establishment, ward hostel, remand shelter, institution or detention centre can be taken under Section 139 for wards, or Section 55 for juvenile offenders of the 1939 *Child Welfare Act* (NSW). The harbouring of absconding wards is an offence under Section 148 (2) of this Act. New legislation introduced in 1988, the *Children Detention Centre Act*, differentiates between absconding from a ward shelter and escaping from a detention centre. Absconding can be dealt with by the superintendent of the shelter under Section 21 of this Act. Escaping is regarded as more serious and is punishable through court action under Section 33.

7 This shift is clearly stated in various Department of YACS (FACS and now DOCS) *Annual Reports*, beginning from 1980 to the present.

8 See Mica Nava's discussion of feminist critiques of the family in L. Segal, (ed.) *What is to be done about the Family*, Penguin, Harmondsworth, 1983, pp. 65–105. See also Gill Bottomley's discussion of feminist and sociological critiques of the family in Burns, A. Bottomley, G. and Jools, P. (eds) *The Family in the Modern World*, Allen and Unwin, Sydney, 1983, pp. 19–30.

Chapter 6

1 a The rising affluence among the post-war working-class combined with the increasing affordability of leisure to create the teenager consumer and hence the economic basis for markets and goods specifically aimed at youth.

 b The mass production and circulation of popular culture through the post-war emergence of the TV and other forms of electronic media, such as the video and the record, created and reproduced images of youth and style diffused and appropriated in youth culture.

 c The celebration of aggressive masculinity in some youth subcultures arose out of a post-war mentality based on the wartime legitimacy of violence and the absence of fathers.

 d A fourth set of changes leading to the emergence of post-war youth subcultures relates to the sphere of education where an increasing number of young people staying on at school leads to the emergence of adolescent societies—the site of youth culture.

 e A whole range of distinctive styles in dress and music emerged in the post-war period to create the conditions for the emergence of youth subcultures (Clarke *et al.* in Hall and Jefferson, 1975, pp. 17–21)

2 During the five years between the 1976 and 1981 Census, the female population aged between ten and nineteen years in the Campbelltown Local Government Area rose from 4346 to 8038 (Carrington, 1989, pp. 136 and 467)

3 For an insightful discussion of delinquency as having one of its genealogies in the discourse of eugenics see Bessant, 1991.

4 The 1950s film *Rebel Without a Cause*, for example, constructs a

discourse of delinquency around a classless, raceless, timeless category of youth. The film is described by its promoters as a 'heartfelt but disturbing classic that introduced middle-class America to an enemy of its own making: its children'.

5 The mod, for example, 'living on the pulse of the present, resurrected after work only by a fierce devotion to leisure' (Hebdige in Hall *et al.*, 1975, pp. 94) is a youth subculture which has effectively created its own heterotopia. The juxtaposition of time and space in mod subculture with conventional concepts of time and space—of the movement between the conventional space of 9.00 a.m. to 5.00 p.m. at school, work, family—to the underground discos and bars, the all-nighters, the bank holidays, mixed with pill popping and conspicuous consumption, effectively reordered conventional norms of time and space, establishing its own peculiar form of governmentality which operated through the style, music, argot and sociality of mod youth culture.

6 Hebdige (1979) describes bricolage as the juxtaposition of two or more contradictory cultural objects or forms into a collage or pastiche. By taking the safety pin out of its domesticated space and utility and to wear it as a gruesome garment through the nose, alongside fragments of the school uniform and the union jack, defiled and juxtaposed against plastic, leather and pink mop tops, Hebdige claims that punk is the par exemplar cultural form of bricolage (Hebdige, 1979, pp. 107).

7 That is, 'Cheryl has an I.Q. in the upper middle range', 'Cheryl is an under-achiever at school' (Psychological Assessment, 28/11/78). 'Therefore Cheryl has developed a pattern of having her own way, she is quite egocentric in many respects and fails to see why others should determine what she should do'. (Psychological Assessment, 30/3.79)

8 That is, 'Cheryl tends to associate with lesser desirable types in Campbelltown, particularly the Browns'. (Court Report, 5.8.78)

9 That is, 'In view of Cheryl's defiance of any type of authority and lack of acceptance of any type of guidance it is felt that she would not respond effectively to a short period in training. Recommendation: Committal to a Training School for a Minimum of Six Months' (Court Report, 17/11/78). Court Reports are generally authored by district officers. The purpose of the Court Report is to supply to the magistrate, in the form of a recommendation, an expert opinion as to the appropriate means to administer to the child before the court. Of the 200 Court Reports I came across during my empirical investigations, on only five occasions did the presiding magistrate contest the recommendation of the expert put before him/her.

10 Imprisonment, as a strategy of normalisation, has been widely recognised as a failure (Foucault, 1977, pp. 262–5; Asher, 1986, p. xi; Frieberg, Fox and Hogan, 1988, p. 156).

11 That is, 'Cheryl has yet again proved that she cannot keep to conditions placed on her by the Children's Court, and even the District Court'. (Court Report, 14/3/79)

12 That is, 'Recommendation: Committal to an institution for minimum period of six months'. (Court Report, 14/3/79)

13 But even here the practices of government do not conform to any single

source, like the state, capitalism or patriarchy. A multiplicity of discourses about youth as a period of rebelliousness, masculinisation and danger; as a period of consumption, fun and pleasure (Hebdige, 1988) about adolescence as an extended time of innocence, infantilisation, asexuality and vulnerability may be administered through the state apparatus of juvenile justice but their genealogy cannot be said to be reducible to it.

Chapter 6

1 1989 *Children (Care and Protection) Act* (NSW) Section 74/1 instructs the Children's Court not to make an order without first considering assessment reports of the child before it. 1989 *Children (Criminal Proceedings) Act* (NSW) Section 25/1 instructs the court to first consider background reports before sentencing the child before it.

2 Benevolence is the reason given for denying the rights of children before the court access to what is effectively the most important prosecution evidence against them. Section 74 (3) of the *Children (Care and Protection) Act* 1987 states that:

> Nothing in this section requires a copy of the whole or any part of an assessment report to be given to a child or to any other person appearing in the proceedings . . . if in the opinion of the Children's Court, the prejudicial effect of the child being unaware of the information contained in the whole or that part of the report is outweighed by the psychological harm that is likely to be occasioned to the child if the child becomes aware of that information.

3 Relating to 262 court appearances among my sample of fifty-nine girls.

4 I am, of course, referring to the removal of sixty-nine children in NSW and seventy-two in Victoria by the child welfare authorities in the two States from families connected with a religious minority group, which was widely reported in the press. See, for example, *Sydney Morning Herald*, 15 May 1992; 16 May 1992; 29 July 1992; 28 August 1992; 12 September 1992; 2 November 1992; 3 November 1992; *Sun-Herald*, 1 November 1992; *The Age*, 15 May 1992; 16 May 1992; *The Australian*, 15 May 1992.

5 This problem has been partly addressed by the new legislation which differentiates between absconding from a ward shelter and escaping from a detention centre. However, there are still many other avenues for State wards to end up in juvenile detention centres.

6 The new legislation proclaimed on 18 January 1988, replacing the 1939 *Child Welfare Act*, includes the *Children (Care and Protection) Act* 1987; the *Children (Criminal Proceedings) Act* 1987; the *Children (Detention Centres) Act* 1987; and the *Children (Community Service Orders) Act* 1987.

7 I gave evidence before that committee based on my research.

8 See, for example; 'Crime Control means action not kid gloves', *The Daily Telegraph*, 1 September 1987; 'Young Crims: No Cautions', *The Sun*, 1 September 1987; 'Hit Young Offenders Harder', *The Telegraph*, 1 September, 1987.

Bibliography

Alder, C. (1985), 'Theories of Female Delinquency', *Juvenile Delinquency in Australia*, eds P. Borowski and M. Murray, Methuen, Australia

Alder, C., O'Connor, I., Warner, K. and White, R. (1992), *Perceptions of the treatment of juveniles in the legal system*, Report to The National Youth Affairs Research Scheme, National Clearing House for Youth Studies, Hobart

Allen, H. (1987), *Justice Unbalanced: Gender, Psychiatry and Judicial Decisions*, Open University Press, Milton Keynes

Allen, J. (1988), 'The masculinity of criminality and criminology: Interrogating some impasses', *Understanding Crime and Criminal Justice*, eds M. Findlay and R. Hogg, Law Book Co., Sydney

——(1989), 'Men, Crime and Criminology: Recasting the Questions', *International Journal of the Sociology of Law*, vol. 17, pp. 19–39

——1990, *Sex and Secrets: Crimes Involving Australian Women since 1880*, Oxford University Press, Oxford

Amos, V. and Parmar, P. (1984), 'Challenging Imperial Feminism', *Feminist Review*, vol. 17, pp. 3–19

Anderson, R. (1978), *Representation in the Juvenile Court*, Routledge & Kegan Paul, London

Aries, P. (1962), *Centuries of Childhood*, Penguin, Middlesex

Asher, G. (1986), *Custody and Control*, Allen & Unwin, Sydney

Australian Bureau of Statistics (1980), *Social Indicators*, Cat. no. 4101.0, AGPS, Canberra

——(1981), *Census 1981 Characteristics of Persons and Dwellings in Local Government Areas New South Wales*, Parts 1 and 2, AGPS, Sydney

——(1981), *Index of Localities New South Wales*, AGPS, Sydney

——1982, *Australian Families*, Cat. no. 4408.0, AGPS, Canberra

Barcan, A. (1980), *A History of Australian Education*, Oxford University Press, Melbourne

Bargen, J. (1992), 'Going to Court Cap in Hand: A Preliminary Evaluation of a Community Aid Panel', *Current Issues in Criminal Justice*, vol. 4, no. 2, pp. 117–40

Bell, D. (1991), 'Aboriginal Women, Separate Spaces and Feminism', *A Reader In Feminist Knowledge*, ed. S. Gunew, Routledge, London

Bessant, J. (1991), 'Described, Measured and Labelled: Eugenics, Youth Policy and Moral Panic in Victoria in the 1950s', *For Your Own Good: Special Issue of Journal of Australian Studies*, pp 8–28

Biles, D. (1989), *Aboriginal Imprisonment—A Statistical Analysis*, Research Paper no. 6, Royal Commission Into Aboriginal Deaths in Custody, Research Unit, AGPS, Canberra

Blackmore, R. (1989), *The Children's Court and Community Welfare in New South Wales*, Longman Chesire, Melbourne

Bowles, S. and Gintis, H. (1970), *Schooling in Capitalist America*, Routledge, London

Brogden, M., Jefferson, T. and Walklate, S. (1988), *Introducing Police Work*, Unwin Hyman, London

Broom, D. H. and Richmond, K. eds (1982), 'Special Edition: Women and Crime', *Australian and New Zealand Journal of Criminology*, vol. 15, pp. 65–8

Brown, B. (1986), 'Women and crime: the dark figures of criminology' *Economy and Society*, vol. 15, no. 3, pp. 355–402

Bryson, L. (1992), *The Welfare State*, Macmillan, London

Burchell, G. (1979), 'A Note on Juvenile Justice', *Ideology and Consciousness*, vol. 5, pp. 125–35

——(1981), 'Putting the child in its place', *Ideology and Consciousness*, no. 8, pp. 73–96

Burns, A., Bottomley, G. and Jools, P. (1983), *The Family in the Modern World*, Allen & Unwin, Sydney

Burnwood, J. and Fletcher, J. (1980), *Sydney and the Bush*, New South Wales Department of Education, Sydney

Burt, C. (1925), *The Delinquent*, The University of London Press, London

Cain M. (1986), 'Realism, Feminism, Methodology and Law', *International Journal of the Sociology of Law*, vol. 14, pp. 255–67

Campbell, A. (1981), *Girl Delinquents*, Basil Blackwell, Oxford

Carby, H. (1982), 'White woman listen: black feminism and the boundaries of sisterhood', *The Empire Strikes Back*, Centre for Contemporary Cultural Studies, Hutchinson, London

Carlen, P., Hicks, J., O'Dywer, J., Christina, D. and Tchaikovsky, C. 1985, *Criminal Women*, Polity Press, Cambridge

Carlen, P. (1987), 'Out of Care, into Custody: Dimensions and Deconstructions of the State's Regulation of Twenty-two Young Working-Class Women', *Gender, Crime and Justice*, eds P. Carlen and A. Worrel, Open University Press, Milton Keynes

——(1988), *Women, Crime and Poverty*, Open University Press, Milton Keynes

——(1992), 'Criminal women and criminal justice, the limits to, and potential of, feminist and left realist perspectives', *Issues in Realist Criminology*, eds R. Matthews and J. Young, Sage, London

Carrington, K. (1989), *Manufacturing Female Delinquency: A Study of Juvenile Justice*, unpublished PhD thesis, Macquarie University, Sydney

——(1990a), 'Aboriginal Girls and Juvenile Justice: What Justice? White Justice', *Journal For Social Justice Studies*, vol. 3, pp. 1–18

——(1990b), 'Feminist readings of female delinquency', *Law in Context: Special Issue, Feminism, Law and Justice*, vol. 8, no. 2, pp. 5–31

——(1991a), 'The Death of Mark Quayle: Normalising Racial Horror in Country Towns and Hospitals', *Journal for Social Justice Studies*, vol. 4, pp. 161–88

——(1991b), 'Policing Families and Controlling Children', *For Your Own Good: Young People and State Intervention in Australia*, Special Issue of the *Journal of Australian Studies*, eds R. White and B. Wilson, pp. 108–17

Carter, J., Burston, O., Floyd, F. and Stewart, J. (1988), *Mandatory Reporting and Child Abuse*, Brotherhood of St Lawrence, Melbourne

Chesney-Lind, M. (1974), 'Juvenile Delinquency and the Sexualisation of Female Crime', *Psychology Today*, July, pp. 4–7

——(1977), 'Judicial Paternalism and the Female Status Offender', *Crime and Delinquency*, vol. 23, pp. 121–30

Cicourel, A. V. (1969), *The Social Organisation of Juvenile Justice*, Heinneman, London

Chisholm, R. (1988), 'Aboriginal Children and the Placement Principle', *Aboriginal Law Bulletin*, vol. 2, no. 31, pp. 42–6

Clarke, J. (1985), 'Whose Justice? The Politics of Juvenile Control', *International Journal of the Sociology of Law*, vol. 13, pp. 407–21

Clarke, J., Critcher, C. and Johnson, R. eds (1979), *Working Class Culture*, Hutchinson, London

Cohen, A. E. (1956), *Delinquent Boys*, The Free Press, New York

Cohen, S. (1980), *Folk Devils and Moral Panics: The Creation of Mods and Rockers*, Martin Robinson, Oxford

Collison, M. (1980), 'Questions of Juvenile Justice', *Radical Issues in Criminology*, eds P. Carlen and M. Collison, Martin Robinson, Oxford

Connell, R. W., Ashenden, D., Kessler, S. and Dowsett, G. (1982), *Making the Difference*, Allen & Unwin, Sydney

Connell, R.W. (1983), *Which way is up? Essays on class, sex and culture*, Allen & Unwin, Sydney

Corrigan, P. (1979), *Schooling the Smash Street Kids*, Macmillan, London

Cousins, M. (1980), 'Men's Rea: A Note on Sexual Difference, Criminology and the Law', *Radical Issues in Criminology*, eds P. Carlen and M. Collison, Martin Robinson, Oxford

Cowlishaw, G. (1988), *Black, White or Brindle: Race Relations in Rural Australia*, Cambridge University Press, Melbourne

Cunneen, C. (1985), 'Working-Class Boys and Crime', *War/Masculinity*, eds P. Patton and R. Poole, Intervention Publications, Sydney

——(1988), 'The Policing of Public Order', *Understanding Crime and Criminal Justice*, eds M. Findlay and R. Hogg, Law Book Co., Sydney

——(1990), *A Study of Aboriginal Juveniles and Police Violence*, Report

Commissioned by the National Inquiry into Racist Violence, Australian Human Rights and Equal Opportunity Commission, Sydney
——(1992), 'Aboriginal Imprisonment During and Since the Royal Commission Into Aboriginal Deaths In Custody', *Current Issues in Criminal Justice*, vol. 3, no. 3, pp. 353–55

Cunneen, C. and Robb, T. (1987), *Criminal Justice in North-West New South Wales*, NSW Bureau of Crime Statistics and Research, Sydney

Dahl, T. (1986), 'Taking Women as a Starting Point: Building Women's Law', *International Journal of the Sociology of Law*, vol. 14, pp. 239–47

Daly, K. (1989), 'Criminal Justice Ideologies and Practices in Different Voices: Some Feminist Questions about Justice', *International Journal of the Sociology of Law*, vol. 17, pp. 1–18

Donzelot, J. (1979), *The Policing of Families*, Pantheon Books, New York

Deem, R. (1980), *Schooling for Women's Work*, Routledge & Kegan Paul, London

Department of Community Services, (1992) *Issues and Trends in Community Services: Trends in Usage of Different types of Substitute Care In NSW*, Research and Data Analysis Branch Discussion Paper, no. 2

D'Souza, N. (1990), 'Aboriginal Children and Juvenile Justice', *Aboriginal Law Bulletin*, vol. 2, no. 44, pp. 4–5

Edwards, C. and Read, P. eds (1989), *The Stolen Generations*, Doubleday, Sydney

Fielding, J. (1977), 'Female Delinquency', *Delinquency in Australia*, ed. P. Wilson, University of Queensland Press, St Lucia

Flax, J. (1987), 'Postmodernism and Gender Relations in Feminist Theory' *Signs*, vol. 12, pp. 621–33

Fletcher, J. (1975), 'Collarenebri—An Attempt to Integrate Aboriginal Children' *The Leader*, vol. 6, no. 2, pp. 30–6

Foucault, M. (1977), *Discipline and Punish: The birth of the prison*, A. Sheridan, translator, Penguin books, England
——(1981), 'Questions of Method: an interview', *Ideology & Consciousness*, vol. 8, pp. 3–14
——(1986), 'Of Other Spaces', *Diacritics*, Spring, no. 16, pp. 22–7
——(1991), 'On Governmentality', *The Foucault Effect: Studies in Governmentality*, eds C. Gordon, P. Miller and G. Burchell, Harvester Wheatsheaf, London

Frieberg, A., Fox, R. and Hogan, M. (1988), *Sentencing Young Offenders*, The Law Reform Commission Sentencing Research Paper No. 11, Alken Press, Smithfield

Fuss, D. (1989), *Essentially Speaking Feminism, Nature and Difference*, Routledge, London

Gamble, H. (1976), 'Decision Making in the Children's Courts of Sydney', *Australian and New Zealand Journal of Criminology*, vol. 9, pp. 168–97

Gaskell, J. (1978), 'Sex Role Ideology and the Aspirations of High School Girls', *Interchange*, vol. 8, no. 3, pp. 43–53

Garfinkel, H. (1967), *Studies in Ethnomethodology*, Prentice-Hall, Englewood Cliffs, New Jersey

Gayle, F. and Wundersitz, J. (1985), 'Variations in the Over-Representation of Aboriginal Young Offenders in the Criminal Justice System', *Australian Journal of Social Issues*, vol. 20, no. 3, pp. 209–14

——(1987), 'Aboriginal Youth and the Criminal Justice System in South Australia', *Ivory Scales: Black Australia and The Law*, ed. K. Hazelhurst, NSW University Press, Sydney

Gelsthorpe, L. (1986), 'Towards a Skeptical Look at Sexism', *International Journal of the Sociology of Law*, vol. 14, pp. 125–52

——(1989), *Sexism and the Female Offender*, Gower, Aldershot

Griffin, C. (1985), *Typical Girls? Young women from school to the job market*, Routledge & Kegan Paul, London

Giroux, H. A. (1988), *Schooling and the struggle for public life*, University of Minnesota Press, Minneapolis

Giroux, H. A. ed. (1991), *Postmodernism, Feminism and Cultural Politics: Redrawing Educational Boundaries*, State University of New York Press, Albany

Goldstein, J., Freud, A. and Solit, J. (1980), *Beyond the Best Interests of the Child*, Burnett Books, London

Goodall, H. (1988), *The Death of Malcolm Charles Smith: Submission to the Royal Commission Into Aboriginal Deaths In Custody on behalf of the Western Aboriginal Legal Service*, unpublished

——(1990), ' "Saving the Children": Gender and the Colonization of Aboriginal Children in NSW 1788 to 1990', *Aboriginal Law Bulletin*, vol. 2, no. 44, pp. 6–9

Gordon, C. (1991), 'Governmental Rationality', *The Foucault Effect*, eds G. Burchell, C. Gordon and P. Miller, Harvester Wheatsheaf, London

Gore, J. Luke, C. (1992), *Feminisms and Critical Pedagogy*, Routledge, London

Griffin, C. (1985), *Typical Girls? Young Women from School to the Job Market*, Routledge, London

Gross, E. (1986), 'Conclusion: What is Feminist Theory', *Feminist Challenges*, eds C. Pateman and E. Gross, Allen & Unwin, Sydney

——(1989), 'The In(ter)vention of Feminist Knowledges', *Crossing Boundaries: Feminisms and the Critique of Knowledges*, Allen & Unwin, Sydney

Gunew, S. ed. (1991), *A Reader in Feminist Knowledge*, Routledge, London

Hall, S. and Jefferson, T. eds (1975), *Resistance Through Rituals: youth subcultures in postwar Britain*, Hutchinson, London

Hall, S., Critcher, T., Jefferson, T., Clarke, J. and Roberts, B. (1988), *Policing The Crisis*, Macmillan, London

Hampton, R. E. (1979), 'Sex and Sentencing in a Children's Court', *Australian and New Zealand Journal of Criminology*, vol. 12, pp. 12–32

Hancock, L. (1980), 'The myth that females are treated more leniently than males in the juvenile justice system', *Australian and New Zealand Journal of Sociology*, vol. 16, no. 3, pp. 4–14

Hancock, L. and Chesney-Lind, M. (1982), 'Female Status Offenders and

Justice Reforms: An International Perspective', *Australian and New Zealand Journal of Criminology*, vol. 15, pp. 109–22

——(1985), 'Juvenile Justice Legislation and Gender Discrimination', *Juvenile Delinquency In Australia*, eds J. Murray and A. Borowski, Methuen, Australia

Hancock, L. and Hiller, A. (1981), 'The Processing of Juveniles in Victoria', *Women and Crime*, eds S. Mukherjee and J. Scutt, Allen & Unwin, Sydney

Harris, A. P. (1990), 'Race and Essentialism in Feminist Legal Theory', *Standford Legal Review*, vol. 42, pp. 581–616

Harris, R. and Webb, D. (1987), *Welfare, Power and Juvenile Justice*, Tavistock, London

Hawkins, G. (1982), *Resistances to School*, Inner City Education Centre, Sydney

Hebdige, D. 1979, *Subculture: The Meaning of Style*, Methuen, London

——(1988), *Hiding in the Light*, Routledge, London

Heidensohn, F. (1985), *Women and Crime*, Macmillan, London

Henriques, J. (1984), 'Social Psychology and the Politics of Racism', *Changing the Subject*, eds J. Henriques, W. Hollway, C. Urwin, C. Vern and V. Walkerdine, Methuen, London

Hindess, B. (1977), 'The concept of class in Marxist theory and Marxist politics', *The Communist University of London*, ed. J. Bloomfield, Lawrence & Wishart, London

Hirst, P. (1981), 'The Genesis of the Social', *Politics & Power 3*, Routledge & Kegan Paul, London

Hogan, M. (1989), *Equality Before the Law?: Disadvantage and Disservice for children in Administrative Law—The case of Child Welfare and Juvenile Justice*, Paper presented to the Law Council of Australian's 26th Australian Legal Convention, Public Interest Advocacy Centre, Sydney

Hogg, R. (1988), 'Taking Crime Seriously: Left Realism and Australian Criminology', *Understanding Crime and Criminal Justice*, eds M. Findlay and R. Hogg, Law Book Co., Sydney

——(1991), 'Policing and Penality', *Journal for Social Justice Studies*, vol. 4, pp. 1–26

Hogg, R. and Brown, D. (1991), 'Violence, Public Policy and Politics in Australia', *Social Effects of Free Market Policies* , ed. I. Taylor, Harvester Wheatsheaf, London

——(1993), 'Policing Patriarchy: Unwelcomed facts on domestic violence', *Australian Left Review*, no. 144, pp. 8–9

Hogg, R. and Golder, H. (1987), 'Policing in the late nineteenth century', *Policing in Australia: Historical Perspectives*, NSW University Press, Sydney

Hollway, W. (1984), 'Gender difference and the production of subjectivity', *Changing the Subject*, eds J. Henriques, W. Hollway, C. Urwin and V. Walkerdine, Methuen, London

Hooks, B. (1984), *Ain't I a Woman? Black Women and Feminism,* Pluto Press, London

Howe, A. (1987), 'Social Injury Revisited: Towards a Feminist Theory of

160   OFFENDING GIRLS

Social Justice', *International Journal of the Sociology of Law*, vol. 15, pp. 423–38

——(1989), 'Sweet Dreams: Deinstitutionalising Young Women', *Dissenting Opinions: Feminist Explorations in Law and Society*, ed. R. Graycar, Allen & Unwin, Sydney

——(1991), 'Postmodern Penal Politics', *Journal for Social Justice Studies*, vol. 4, pp. 61–72

Humphries, S. (1981), *Hooligans or Rebels*, Basil Blackwell, Oxford

Hunter, I. (1988), 'Setting Limits to Culture' *New Formations*, no. 4, Spring, pp. 103–21

Johnson, E. (1991), *National Report*, vols 1–5, Royal Commission Into Aboriginal Deaths In Custody, AGPS, Canberra

Johnson, M. (1970), *Derbyshire Village Schools in the Nineteenth Century*, David & Charles, Devon

Johnson, R. (1976), 'Notes on the Schooling of the English Working Class', *Schooling Under Capitalism*, eds R. Dale, G. Esland and M. MacDonald, Routledge & Kegan Paul, London

Jones, M. A. (1985), *Social Welfare in Australia*, Allen & Unwin, Sydney

Juvenile Justice Advisory Council (1993), *Green Paper: Future Directions for Juvenile Justice in New South Wales*, Government Printers, Sydney

Kenway, J. (1985), 'On the "Innocence" of Ideology', *Australian Journal of Cultural Studies*, vol. 3, no. 2, pp. 151–61

Laurie, V. (1992), 'Victims: Crime and Prejudice in the West', *The Australian Magazine*, November 7–8, pp. 14–20

Lees, S. (1986), *Losing Out: Adolescent Girls & Sexuality*, Hutchinson, London

Maher, L. and Waring, E. J. (1989), 'Beyond Simple Differences: White Collar Crime, Gender and Workforce Position', *Phoebe*, Spring, vol. 2, no. 1, pp. 44–54

May, D. (1977), 'Delinquent Girls Before the Courts' *Medicine, Science and the Law*, vol. 17, no. 3, pp. 203–12

McConnochie, K. R. (1982), 'Aborigines and Australian Education: Historical Perspectives', *Aboriginal Education*, ed. J. Sherwood, Creative Research, Perth

McCorquodale, J. (1987), *Aborigines and the Law: A Digest*, Aboriginal Studies Press, Canberra

McDonald, D. (1990), *National Police Custody Survey August 1988*, Research Paper No. 13, Royal Commission into Aboriginal Deaths in Custody, Research Unit, AGPS, Canberra

MacDonald, M. (1980), 'Schooling and the Reproduction of Class and Gender Relations', *Schooling, Ideology and the Curriculum*, eds L. Barton and R. Meighan, Falmer Press, England

MacKinnon, C. A. (1983), 'Feminism, Marxism, Method and the State: Toward a Feminist Jurisprudence', *Signs*, vol. 8, no. 4, pp. 635–58

McRobbie, A. 1978, 'Working-Class Girls and the Culture of Femininity', *Women Take Issue*, eds Women's Studies Group, Centre for Contemporary Cultural Studies, Hutchinson, London

——(1991), *Feminism and Youth Culture*, Macmillan, London

Miles, I. and Irvine, I. (1979), 'The critique of Official Statistics', *Demys-*

tifying Social Statistics, eds I. Irvine, I. Miles and J. Evans, Pluto Press, London

Morris, A., Giller, H., Szwed, E. and Geach, H. (1980), *Justice For Children*, Macmillan, London

Morris, B. (1989), *Domesticating Resistance: The Dhan-gadi Aborigines and the Australian State*, Burg Press, Oxford

Mowbray, M. (1992), 'The political economy of substitute care: developments in Child Welfare in New South Wales', *Caring* vol. 16, no. 3, pp. 4–12

Mukherjee, S. (1984), *Age and Crime*, Australian Institute of Criminology, Canberra

Muirhead, J. (1989), *Interim Report*, Royal Commission Into Aboriginal Deaths In Custody, AGPS, Canberra

Naffine, N. (1986), 'Women and Crime', *Australian Criminal Justice Systems—The Mid-1980s*, eds D. Chappel and P. Wilson, Butterworths, Sydney

Naffine, N. (1987), *Female Crime: The construction of women in criminology*, Allen & Unwin, Sydney

New South Wales Department of Child Welfare (1970), *Child Welfare In New South Wales*, AGPS, NSW

New South Wales Department of Youth and Community Services, 1960 to 1990 *Annual Reports*, AGPS, Sydney

Omedie, R. A. (1979), 'Delinquency in Girls in South Australia', *Australian and New Zealand Journal of Sociology*, vol. 15, no. 1, pp. 81–85

Pasquino, P. (1991), 'Theatrum Politicum', *The Foucault Effect*, eds G. Burchell, C. Gordon and P. Miller, Harvester Wheatsheaf, London

Payne, S. (1992), 'Aboriginal Women and the Law', *Aboriginal Perspectives on Criminal Justice*, Institute of Criminology Monograph Series no. 1, The Institute of Criminology, Sydney

Pearson, G. (1983), *Hooligan: A History of Respectable Fears*, Macmillan, London

Pratt, J. (1989), 'Corporatism: The Third Model of Juvenile Justice', *British Journal of Criminology*, vol. 29, no. 3, pp. 236–54

Proceedings of the National Association for the Promotion of Social Science, 1857, London

Ramsland, J. (1986), *Children of the Backlanes: Destitute and Neglected Children in Colonial New South Wales*, NSW University Press, Sydney

Read, P. (undated), *The Stolen Generations: The Removal of Aboriginal Children in N.S.W. 1883 to 1969*, Occasional Paper No. 1, New South Wales Ministry for Aboriginal Affairs, Sydney

Report of the Senate Standing Committee on Social Welfare(1985), *Children in Institutional and Other Forms of Care: A National Perspective*, AGPS, Canberra

Robbins, D. Cohen, P. (1978), *Knuckle Sandwich*, Penguin Books, Middlesex

Rose, N. (1985), *The Psychological Complex*, Routledge, London

——(1987), 'Beyond the Public/Private Division: Law, Power and the Family', *Journal of Law and Society*, vol. 14, no. 1, pp. 61–76

——(1989), *Governing the Soul*, Routledge, London

Sarri, R. C. (1976), 'Juvenile Law: How it Penalises Females', *The Female Offender*, ed. Crites, L., Lexington Books, Lexington

Shacklady Smith, L. (1978), 'Sexist Assumptions and Female Delinquency', *Women, Sexuality and Social Control*, eds C. Smart and B. Smart, Routledge & Kegan Paul, London

Scholossman, S. and Wallach, S. (1978), 'The Crime of Precocious Female Sexuality: Female Juvenile Delinquency in the Progressive Era', *Harvard Educational Review*, vol. 48, no. 1, pp. 65–94

Schwichtenberg, C. (1993), 'Madonna's postmodern feminism', *The Madonna Connection*, Allen & Unwin, Sydney

Segal, L. ed. (1983), *What Is To Be Done About The Family?*, Penguin, Harmondsworth

Sharp, R. (1980), *Knowledge, Ideology and Politics of Schooling*, Routledge & Kegan Paul, London

Sherwood, J. ed. (1982), *Aboriginal Education*, Creative Research, Perth

Slee, R. ed. (1992), *Discipline in Australian Public Education*, ACER, Hawthorn

Smart, C. (1976), *Women, Crime & Criminology*, Routledge & Kegan Paul, London

——(1986), 'Feminism and Law: Some Problems of Analysis and Strategy', *International Journal of the Sociology of Law*, vol. 14, pp. 109–23

——(1989), *Feminism and the Power of Law*, Routledge, London

Standing Committee on Social Issues (1992), *Juvenile Justice in New South Wales*, Standing Committee on Social Issues Report no. 4, Parliament of New South Wales Legislative Council, AGPS, Sydney

Standing Committee of Social Welfare Administrators (1992), *Children Under Care and Protection Orders: National Data Collection 1989–1990*, (Welstat, The Standardisation of Social Welfare Statistics Project), Department of Community Services, Ashfield

Stratten, J. (1992), *The Young Ones: Working-class Culture, Consumption and the Category of Youth*, Black Swan Press, Perth

Sweeney, T. (1989), 'Inequalities in our Provision For Young Children', *Australian Welfare: Historical Sociology*, ed. R. Kennedy, Macmillan, Melbourne

Tait, G. (1992), 'Reassessing Street Kids: A critique of subculture theory', *Youth Studies Australia*, vol. 11, no. 2, pp 12–18

Terry, R. M. (1970), 'Discrimination in the handling of juvenile offenders by social control agencies', *Becoming Delinquent*, eds P. G. Garabedian and D. C. Gibbons, Aldine, Chicago

Tolsen, A. (1990), 'Social Surveillance and Subjectification: the Emergence of "Subculture" in the work of Henry Mayhew', *Cultural Studies*, vol. 4, no. 2, pp. 113–17

Transactions of the International Penitentiary Congress (1872), *Prisons and Reformatories at Home and Abroad*, London, July 3–13

Tyler, D. (1983), 'The Development of the Concept of Juvenile Delinquency', *Melbourne Working papers*, eds R. Tese and G.

Wickham, Sociology Research Group in Cultural and Educational Studies, Melbourne University, Melbourne

——(1986), 'The case of Irene Tuckerman: understanding sexual violence and the protection of women and girls, Victoria 1890–1925', *History of Education Review*, vol. 15, no. 2, pp. 52–67

Usher, J. (1992), *Review of substitute services*, (Report to the Minister for Health and Community Services), Sydney

Van Kreiken, R. (1991), *Children and the State*, Allen & Unwin, Sydney

Van Swaaningen, R. (1989), 'Feminism and Abolitionism as Critiques of Criminology', *International Journal of the Sociology of Law*, vol. 17, pp. 287–306

Waldby, C. (1985), *Breaking the Silence*, Women Against Incest Collective, Sydney

Watson, I. (1985), *Double Depression, Schooling, Unemployment and Family Life in the Eighties*, George Allen & Unwin, Sydney

White, R. (1990), *No Space of Their Own: Young people and social control in Australia*, Cambridge, Sydney

Wickham, G. ed. (1987), *Social Theory and Legal Politics*, Local Consumption Publications, Sydney

——(1992), 'Towards a sociology of Governance,' Paper presented at The Australian Sociological Association Conference, Murdoch University, Perth

Willis, P. (1977), *Learning to Labour*, Saxton House/Gower, London

Wilson, E. (1988), *Western Aboriginal Legal Service Submission to the Royal Commission Into Aboriginal Deaths in Custody*, unpublished

Wilson, P. (1988), *Beyond the Political Rhetoric of the Law and Order Debate*, Unpublished paper presented to a public meeting convened by the Campaign for Criminal Justice

Wootten, H. (1989), *Report on the Death of Malcolm Charles Smith*, The Royal Commission into Aboriginal Deaths in Custody, AGPS, Canberra

——(1991), *Regional Report of Inquiry in New South Wales, Victoria and Tasmania*, Royal Commission Into Aboriginal Deaths in Custody, AGPS, Canberra

Young, G. M. (1965), *Portrait of an Age*, 2nd edn, Oxford University Press, London

Youth Justice Coalition (1990), *Kids In Justice: a blue print for the 90s*, A Project of the Youth Justice Coalition NSW, Youth Justice Coalition, Sydney

Index